Praying

THROUGH THE

NAMES OF THE

Holy
Spirit

TONY EVANS

HARVEST HOUSE PUBLISHERS
EUGENE. OREGON

Cover design by Faceout Studios

Cover images © marukopum, Sentavio / Shutterstock

Interior design by KUHN Design Group

The prayers in this book were inspired by Dr. Evans' teaching but were written with the help of his writing assistant, Heather Hair.

For bulk, special sales, or ministry purchases, please call 1-800-547-8979.
Email: CustomerService@hhpbooks.com

This logo is a federally registered trademark of the Hawkins Children's LLC. Harvest House Publishers, Inc., is the exclusive licensee of this trademark.

Praying Through the Names of the Holy Spirit
Copyright © 2023 by Tony Evans
Published by Harvest House Publishers
Eugene, Oregon 97408
www.harvesthousepublishers.com

ISBN 978-0-7369-8449-2 (pbk)
ISBN 978-0-7369-8450-8 (eBook)

Library of Congress Control Number: 2023947077

Printed in the United States of America

24 25 26 27 28 29 30 31 32 / BP / 10 9 8 7 6 5 4 3 2 1

ACKNOWLEDGMENTS

I want to thank Harvest House Publishers for their partnership on this book, especially Kim Moore for leading their team in this process. I also want to thank my collaborative writer, Heather Hair, for her work in creating these prayers as well as the prayers in my other prayer books with Harvest House throughout the years:

Prayers for Knowing God

Prayers for Victory in Spiritual Warfare

Prayers for Victory in Your Marriage

Praying like a Kingdom Hero

Praying Through the Names of God

Praying Through the Names of Jesus

Contents

Journeying Through the Holy Spirit's Names in Prayer...9

1. The Helper...13

2. The Dove...15

3. The Living Water...17

4. The Anointing...19

5. The Spirit of the Lord...21

6. The Wine...23

7. The Fruit...25

8. The Intercessor...27

9. The Pledge of Our Inheritance...29

10. The Breath...31

11. The Power...33

12. The Wind...35

13. The Spirit of Wisdom...37

14. The Spirit of Counsel...39

15. The Spirit of Knowledge...41

16. The Spirit of Truth...45

17. The Advocate Who Testifies...47

18. The Spirit of God...49

19. The Dweller in the Temple...51

20. The Spirit of the Sovereign Lord...53

21. The Spirit of Supplication...57

22. The Spirit of Grace...61

23. The Spirit of Holiness...63

24. The Spirit of Christ...67

25. The Spirit Who Guides Our Way...69

26. The Spirit of Glory...71

27. The Spirit of Revelation...73

28. The Spirit of Adoption...75

29. The Spirit of Faith...77

30. The Eternal Spirit...81

31. The Spirit of Renewal...85

32. The Spirit of Judgment and Burning...87

33. The Spirit Who Searches the Depths of God...91

34. The Spirit of Justice...95

35. The New Spirit...99

36. The Spirit Who Gives Rest...103

37. The Spirit Who Blows like the Wind...107

38. The Spirit Who Knows God's Thoughts...109

39. The Spirit Who Testifies We Are God's Children...113

40. The Spirit Who Heals...117

41. The Spirit of Fire...121

42. The Spirit Flowing Within...125

43. The Spirit from God...127

44. The Spirit of Life...129

45. The Holy Spirit Power of the Most High...131

46. The Spirit Who Seals...135

47. The Spirit Who Washes, Sanctifies, and Justifies...137

48. The Spirit of Power, Love, and Discipline...141

49. The Promise...143

50. The Spirit of Prophecy...145

51. The Spirit Who Abides in You...147

52. The Holy Spirit of God...149

53. The Spirit Who Instructs...151

54. The Spirit of Jesus Christ...153

55. The First Fruits of the Spirit...155

56. The Spirit of Strength...157

57. The Spirit Who Seeks the Will of God...159

58. The Filling Spirit...161

59. The Spirit Who Distributes Gifts...163

60. The Spirit Who Walks with You...165

APPENDIX A:
A Look at the Fruit of the Spirit...169

APPENDIX B:
The Urban Alternative...175

Journeying Through the Holy Spirit's Names in Prayer

The power of the Holy Spirit is available to each of us, and yet He's often the most overlooked and underutilized Person of the Trinity. The Holy Spirit was sent to minister to us, convict us, teach us, give us insight into God's depth, enable us to live a life of love and joy, and much more. We can come to know all the ways He's available to us as we pray to God concerning the various roles He intends for the Holy Spirit to manifest in us and through us.

In this book, I've provided guided prayers that appeal to 60 names of the Holy Spirit, all found in Scripture. To get to know His names more deeply is to better understand how the Holy Spirit has been sent to work in your life. Praying each prayer introduces you to aspects of the Holy Spirit's role and allows you to gain greater wisdom into His attributes and purposes. He works within believers' lives in a number of unique ways, but sometimes we forget them. I hope this book reminds you to call on the Holy Spirit and look to Him to help you in times of need. I also want you to draw closer to the Holy Spirit as you come to know Him in a broader way.

Each name or attribute sheds light on who the Holy Spirit is, how He can relate to you, and how He can bless you. As you pray prayers that reflect these qualities of the Holy Spirit, you become more familiar with how He can bring you peace, hope, restraint, and so many of the Christian kingdom virtues.

To help you know how to pray along the lines of the Holy Spirit's many names and roles, you'll find four prayers related to each name or role included in this book. Prayer is heavenly permission for earthly interference. Prayer is communication with God. God longs to be involved with you on a very personal level, and prayer opens the door for this to happen. And I encourage you to pray these prayers so you can come to know the Holy Spirit in a fresh and engaging way.

Feel free to use them either verbatim or simply as a starting point for your own prayers. Whatever you do, be sure to pray them from your heart with meaning, reverence, and authenticity. It doesn't matter so much how you use these prayers. What matters most is that you do pray and make prayer a regular occurrence in your life.

Each set of prayers, as in my books *Praying Through the Names of God* and *Praying Through the Names of Jesus*, is based on the prayer acronym ACTS. This prayer acronym isn't a magic formula. Rather, it's a structure wherein our prayers can cover four important aspects of communication with the Lord—Adoration, Confession, Thanksgiving, and Supplication.

I also want you to use these prayers to help you focus more intently on your abiding relationship with God, the Father, and with Jesus, our Lord, through the inner working of the Holy Spirit. As you do, you can follow this helpful outline:

> **Identify** a time when you can spend concentrated and focused energy on Jesus each day. The book of John calls this "abiding."

Consider several ways to nurture your relationship with God through the presence of the Holy Spirit. It could be freely writing any thoughts you have toward Him in a journal or meditating on Scripture on the Holy Spirit for a few minutes. Scripture is included with each of the 60 Holy Spirit's names in this book to help you with this.

Evaluate how your relationship with the Holy Spirit deepens as you spend consistent time with Him and acknowledge His place in your life. Also evaluate whether it becomes easier to look to the Holy Spirit for His help and presence when you need Him.

Repeat this practice. After you've put this practice into play for a week, seek to repeat it in the weeks to come. You can incorporate these prayers into your daily intimate time with God.

The Holy Spirit is a gift from God sent to enable you to live out the kingdom life. In Him, you can find comfort, help, wisdom, contentment, insight, and so much more. Knowing and praying through the Holy Spirit's names may also bring stability in many areas of your life, including emotional health, spiritual maturity, kingdom virtues, and personal strength.

May the Lord use these prayers to draw you closer to Him so that you come to know Him as your Abba—your Father—through the abiding work and ministry of the Holy Spirit.

1

The Helper

I will ask the Father, and He will give you another Helper,
that He may be with you forever.

JOHN 14:16

ADORATION

Father, thank You for the gift of the Holy Spirit. I adore You, and I honor Your name as I seek Your will in my life. I ask that You show me how to pray through the names of the Holy Spirit in a way that brings You honor and glory.

Throughout my days, remind me to lean on the Holy Spirit. Remind me of the greatness of Your love in providing a Helper to come alongside me when I need Him the most. Help me always remember to put You first in all things as a reflection of my heart's adoration of You. I marvel at how You've made plans from the beginning. I marvel at how You've provided for each of us in our own unique ways. I'm not a random being to You—You know my name and what I need even before I ask You for it.

CONFESSION

God, I confess that far too often I try to solve my problems on my own. Perhaps I forget the Holy Spirit is there because I don't see Him in tangible form. Or I want to rely on myself so I can feel self-sufficient. There are many reasons why I might rely on myself rather than on You.

Help me understand those reasons so I can address them. I confess that I don't look to You for help as much as I can or should through the power and presence of the Holy Spirit, so I ask that You have mercy on me. Gently nudge me in the right direction for Your glory and the advancement of Your kingdom on this earth.

THANKSGIVING

Thank You, Father, for the help You give me through the presence and gift of the Holy Spirit. Thank You that I don't need to face the trials of life alone. When I'm afraid, I can look to You to guide and direct me. Your guidance comes through the Holy Spirit, who is my Helper.

I give You thanks from all of my heart, knowing how awful it would be to go through life on my own. I need Your Spirit's help in so many ways. Just knowing that You've offered Him to me as my Helper fills my soul with gratitude and thanksgiving.

SUPPLICATION

Lord God, I need Your help. But more than that, I need to know how to best access Your help through the power and presence of the Holy Spirit.

Please teach me how to look to the Spirit on a more regular and natural basis. Show me what it means to rely on the Spirit's help and be refreshed and renewed by it. Give me spiritual insight into the working of the Spirit in my soul so that I won't go through life ignoring or underutilizing the Spirit's strength and help, especially when I need it most. Help me understand why You've given me the Spirit in the first place and how I can benefit from His presence in me.

The Dove

*After being baptized, Jesus came
up immediately from the water;
and behold, the heavens were opened,
and He saw the Spirit of God
descending as a dove and lighting on Him.*

MATTHEW 3:16

ADORATION

Father, Your plan for all humanity involves a complex set of circumstances—a set that includes the sending of Your Son, Jesus Christ, to be our sacrifice. But when Jesus left to return to heaven, You knew we needed His presence with us, so You sent the Holy Spirit.

I praise You for thinking of all that we need and providing it. I praise You for knowing what I need before I do and supplying it through the form of the Holy Spirit and His presence in me. I worship You for Your wisdom in how You've set up this world to function so that sinful humanity can come to personally know the Holy One through the connection given us with the Holy Spirit. His presence is like a dove— close, gentle, and secure.

CONFESSION

God, I confess my sin of at times trying to make the Holy Spirit into something He's not. I confess that at other times I ignore the Spirit's presence in my life. Maybe when I feel the Spirit is too gentle, and so I take on my issues or problems myself. Or maybe I neglect to appreciate the gifts of the Spirit in the form of a dove.

The dove symbolized Your pleasure, Your acceptance, and Your anointing power and plan. Help me focus on the meaning of the dove when it reflects the Holy Spirit in my life.

THANKSGIVING

Father, thank You for loving me enough to give me Your pleasure, Your acceptance, and Your anointing power when I have the presence of the Holy Spirit in me. Thank You for gifting me with the gentleness of the dove within. Thank You for not only showing up as the kingdom warrior or sovereign Lord, but in the gentleness of a dove, bringing comfort, beauty, and delight to me.

Thank You for allowing me to see all sides of You through the manifestation of the Holy Spirit inside my spirit and His speaking to me on Your behalf.

SUPPLICATION

Lord God, I ask that You bring me peace through the dove of Your Holy Spirit. I ask that You quiet my anxiety and discomfort with the Spirit's presence. Heal my grief and bring calm to the chaos swirling both within and without me, and let that calm come through the presence of the Holy Dove.

I receive the Spirit's healing peace, and I choose to allow Him to make His place at home in my soul, permeating my mind with thoughts of comfort, trust, faith, and hope. I ask You to remind me of the power of the Dove and the peace He has to offer, especially when I'm struggling with pain and loss.

The Living Water

*On the last day, the great day of the feast, Jesus stood
and cried out, saying, "If anyone is thirsty, let him
come to Me and drink. He who believes in Me, as the
Scripture said, 'From his innermost being will flow rivers
of living water.'" But this He spoke of the Spirit, whom
those who believed in Him were to receive; for the Spirit
was not yet given, because Jesus was not yet glorified.*

JOHN 7:37-39

ADORATION

Father, Your plan to supply all that I need through the presence of
the Holy Spirit covers all the ways I need to be provided for. You even
thought of caring for me by giving me access to an ongoing supply of
living water through the Spirit.

When Jesus spoke of this living water, the Spirit had not yet been
given. He could only speak of what was to come. The disciples could
only hope for a day they had not yet experienced. But I'm living in the
time when the presence of the living water can rest in me. Your Holy
Spirit rests in me, flowing to me as the living water, and I praise You
and thank You for this.

CONFESSION

God, I understand what I need to do when my physical body is thirsty. I understand the impact thirst or dehydration has on it. I know to get a drink and rehydrate or else I'll feel pain and suffering.

And yet, Lord, I confess that I don't always approach the Holy Spirit for the living water He can supply, even when my spirit is thirsty. I remain spiritually thirsty far too long. I look elsewhere for water, from the world, but that water will never satisfy me. Forgive me for failing to fully access the living water You've provided for me each day, especially in my times of greatest need.

THANKSGIVING

Father, thank You for the living water that is the Holy Spirit and the life given me and my spirit through this living water. Thank You for refreshing my spirit with Your living water and nourishing my soul with that which will bring me strength and vitality.

Revitalize my soul with Your presence, and let me know the closeness of Your Spirit in all I do. Thank You that I can easily find refreshment in the Holy Spirit, who supplies living water to me.

SUPPLICATION

Lord God, I ask for the living water of the Holy Spirit to flow through me, bringing me refreshment and strengthening my soul with its presence. Show me how to access more of the living water on a regular basis so that I can be free to benefit from this source of life within me. Let me feel the grace flowing through me as I rest in Your Spirit's provision so that my innermost being is refreshed by the Spirit's innermost being.

Let me also be a light, encouragement, and strength to others when they're in need, pointing them toward the Spirit and His power to bring refreshment and life to all He touches.

4

The Anointing

As for you, the anointing which you received from
Him abides in you, and you have no need for anyone
to teach you; but as His anointing teaches you
about all things, and is true and is not a lie, and
just as it has taught you, you abide in Him.

1 JOHN 2:27

ADORATION

Father, Your will is perfect, and Your way reaches beyond my understanding. I worship You and adore You for how you've made all things perfect in their own time. I look to You when I don't feel capable or able to fulfill the will and calling You've placed on my life.

But I also know You're preparing me for what's ahead. You're making the way possible so that the anointing can show up and manifest Your glory to a world that needs You so much. I love You and give You all of my praise and love, Father.

CONFESSION

God, I confess that I often feel unqualified to fulfill the plans You have for me. I think I may not know all of the right things to say or have all of the skills I need. But, Lord, time and time again You remind me that Your will is not carried out by my own strength. Rather, it's by the anointing of Your Holy Spirit upon me.

I thank You for this, and I ask that You forgive me for when I've fallen short, failing to step out in courage to live out the life You've planned for me to pursue.

THANKSGIVING

Father, thank You for giving me the grace that comes from the anointing available to me through the presence of Your Holy Spirit. Thank You for having a great plan for my life, where I can be of positive impact to those around me. I want to show others Your love, and I thank You for giving me the opportunity to do that through the life You've blessed me to enjoy.

Thank You for the purpose You had in mind when You chose to form me in my mother's womb. I trust You to fulfill this purpose as I commit my life to serving and honoring You.

SUPPLICATION

Lord God, help me tap into the power and beauty of the anointing of the Holy Spirit. Help me understand Your will so that I can experience it more fully. Place Your anointing power within me so deeply that I can tap into the courage and strength the Spirit has to supply.

Help me see the good You're bringing about as You touch my heart and mind with the Spirit. Help me speak the right words in season to whomever needs to hear them. Make me an instrument of comfort and care as You lead me with the wisdom of the Holy Spirit's anointing in me.

5

The Spirit of the Lord

The Lord is the Spirit,
and where the Spirit of the Lord is, there is liberty.
2 CORINTHIANS 3:17

ADORATION

Father, You've created our world with such grandeur and beauty. You've made Your creation a testament to Your power and might. Everywhere I look, I see You, and I delight in what You've made.

I worship You for Your great power. I adore You for Your great might. I honor You, for Your hand is over all and above all. No one is higher and more powerful than You. Where Your Spirit is, You are reflected, and You are glorified.

CONFESSION

God, I confess that I often go through my days focused on myself and miss the grandeur of Your creation. And I confess that I often look at what I've lost rather than what I have or what I can enjoy.

I ask for Your forgiveness in neglecting to praise and honor You as I should and as You deserve. Your Spirit gives liberty, and yet in this liberty, I sometimes respond only in selfishness or in my own self-interests, neglecting the God who gave me the liberty to begin with. Forgive me for failing to give You the honor and praise You deserve for the freedom You've given me to enjoy my life.

THANKSGIVING

Father, thank You for liberty. Thank You for grace. Thank You that the Spirit has set me free from fear and the bondage of legalism. Thank You that You trust me and want to see me flourish.

You are a loving, kind, caring God, and I thank You for the gift of Your Spirit and His presence in my life. Thank You for helping me recognize Your hand more and more each day so that I can be drawn to You in gratitude and praise on a more consistent basis. I love You and thank You for the liberty Your Spirit freely gives me.

SUPPLICATION

Lord God, I ask that I not use the liberty You've graced me with through Your Spirit in a way that would cause You disappointment. I ask that, instead, I use the liberty in a way that brings You great joy.

Give me wisdom on what to do with my time and how to be a more effective kingdom disciple so that I can help advance Your kingdom agenda on earth. I want to make Your name known and to glorify You in all that I do, so I ask that You guide my steps and direct me in the path that brings You the greatest glory and other people the most good.

6

The Wine

Nor do people put new wine into old wineskins;
otherwise the wineskins burst, and the wine pours
out and the wineskins are ruined; but they put new
wine into fresh wineskins, and both are preserved.

MATTHEW 9:17

ADORATION

Father, Your wisdom reminds me that I shouldn't rely on my flesh when it comes to living the spiritual life. In Your Word, You remind me that we're not to put new wine into old wineskins. My flesh and the world's wisdom tied to it is like an old wineskin. But when I live and operate according to the Holy Spirit, I need to receive His grace and peace into my new spirit birthed within through the shed blood of Jesus Christ.

I praise You for the wisdom You give in Your Word. I praise You for allowing me access to Your Word so that I do not have to guess how to live my life wisely.

CONFESSION

God, I confess that I sometimes try to push the Spirit's wisdom down into my fleshly thoughts, only to have everything turn into a mess. But I can't merge my thoughts with Your thoughts. I can't merge worldly wisdom with godly wisdom. I can only look to You and the newness of Your Holy Spirit to provide me with what I need to live a holy and God-honoring life.

Forgive me for when I seek my own way rather than rely on You and Your Spirit to give me all I need regarding how to live my life.

THANKSGIVING

Father, thank You for the newness the Holy Spirit gives me—the new thoughts, new ways to perceive, and new wisdom found in Your Word. Thank You for the newness of life that comes through knowing the Spirit and His eternal love. Thank You for blessing me with His grace in all things.

I want to honor the Spirit's place in my life through inviting Him into all of my thoughts and decisions. Thank You for giving me the opportunity to do this, showing me all I need to lead a truly kingdom-minded life.

SUPPLICATION

Lord God, I ask for reminders in those times and seasons when I seek to combine the newness of the Holy Spirit's presence with the oldness of my flesh and thoughts. Gently remind me so that I can adjust my thoughts and realign myself with Your kingdom purpose.

I ask for the renewing of my mind so my thoughts will be more in tune with Yours. I want to walk in the fullness of life Jesus Christ came to supply. Enable me to do that as I turn to the Holy Spirit to guide me and lead me along the way. Show me what it means to put new wine into new wineskins. Show me what it means to live a new-wineskin kind of life that brings You honor and pleases You in all things.

7

The Fruit

*The fruit of the Spirit is love, joy, peace, patience,
kindness, goodness, faithfulness, gentleness, self-
control; against such things there is no law.*

GALATIANS 5:22-23

ADORATION

Father, Your fruit is evident in all that You do. You are a God of love.
You shower love on me every day and in a myriad of ways. You are a
God of joy. Your joy lights up the sky with the warmth of the sun. You
are a God of peace. Your peace permeates my mind and heart, especially
when I need it most.

You are a God of patience. Your patience keeps Your wrath from giving me what I deserve. You are a God of kindness. Your kindness reveals
to me all I have to be grateful for. You are a God of goodness, faithfulness, gentleness, self-control, and so much more. I praise You for who
You are, and I honor Your name.

CONFESSION

God, I confess that I don't always reflect Your fruit You've made available to me through the process of walking with the Spirit. I confess that I'm not always a person of love and kindness even though I should be. Perhaps I'm trying too hard in my own strength rather than relying on You and Your Spirit in me.

Show me how to honor You better and more fully in all I do by my walking more closely in the power of the Holy Spirit. When I do that, I'll bring You greater joy, and I'll reflect Your image to those around me.

THANKSGIVING

Father, thank You for the fruit of the Spirit made manifest in other people's lives. Thank You for all of the times I get to experience You more fully by experiencing other people who reflect You. Thank You for Your Spirit's work in others, which gives me the opportunity to come into contact with love, joy, peace, patience, kindness, goodness, faithfulness, gentleness, and self-control.

Thank You also for giving me the opportunity to reflect all of these character qualities from You to others. I want to represent You in all I do, say, and think so that I honor You and advance Your kingdom agenda.

SUPPLICATION

Lord God, I want to resemble You more than I do. I want to know Your presence more closely by walking so consistently in Your Spirit that Your Spirit reflects Your love in and through me. Help me be a representative of Your kingdom by living out the fruit of the Spirit, whether or not I feel like doing so. Help me put You first by choosing the fruit of the Spirit over the fruit of my flesh.

I release jealousy, anger, lust, and unforgiveness, knowing these don't honor You. I ask that, instead, You fill me with all I need to live a life that resembles the fruit of the Spirit everywhere I go.

8

The Intercessor

*The Spirit also helps our weakness; for we do not
know how to pray as we should, but the Spirit Himself
intercedes for us with groanings too deep for words.*

ROMANS 8:26

ADORATION

Father, Your language and words are different from mine. The way You
speak is different from the way I speak. When I pray to You, I don't
know the words You naturally hear. That's why You've given the Spirit
as my Intercessor.

I praise You for desiring to communicate with me so much that You've
supplied an Intercessor. You are a mighty God, and You've brought me
such amazing joy just knowing that You care enough about me to give
me an Intercessor so we can speak together freely. I thank You for all
Your gifts, which are many.

CONFESSION

God, I confess that I don't rely on the Holy Spirit as my Intercessor as
much as I could. I confess that I often think I know how to communicate

my thoughts, desires, wants, and needs to You rather than asking the Spirit to translate for me. The Spirit can search the depths of my spirit to uncover what I may not even know to pray for or about. But how often do I invite the Spirit to do so?

May I be forgiven for failing to use the gift of the Holy Spirit at the level You intended when You gave Him to me.

THANKSGIVING

Father, thank You for knowing and understanding me so much better than I know and understand myself. In this way, You can intercede for what my soul desires and truly longs for. I sometimes don't know what to pray for or what to say in my prayers. I get confused by all the world's chatter and the thoughts in my own mind, and it becomes difficult to discern my true spiritual needs.

But You know what they are, and You've supplied me with the Holy Spirit, who prays for me with words and groanings I don't even know how to interpret. Thank You for giving me this gift of the Holy Spirit and everything I gain from tapping into His ability to intercede on my behalf.

SUPPLICATION

Lord God, I ask that the Spirit would intercede for me right now. I'm in the midst of great pain and unknowing, and I need spiritual clarity for my purpose in life and how to heal from past pain. Will You bless me with the Holy Spirit interceding on my behalf, asking You for what I need the most?

I desire what will bring me true spiritual development and make me a better kingdom ambassador for You in all that I do. I also ask that I feel and experience the Holy Spirit praying on my behalf—that somehow You'll help me recognize what the Holy Spirit is doing so I can be more grateful, as I should. I ask that You glorify Yourself through the work You're doing in my life and that I will see Your glory more fully.

9

The Pledge of Our Inheritance

In Him, you also, after listening to the message of truth, the gospel of your salvation—having also believed, you were sealed in Him with the Holy Spirit of promise, who is given as a pledge of our inheritance, with a view to the redemption of God's own possession, to the praise of His glory.

EPHESIANS 1:13-14

ADORATION

Father, Your glory is to be praised. Your glory is to be recognized. Your glory is to be revered, honored, and adored. I worship You because You're a God of great glory. You've created the world and all it contains, and You've placed Your seal of the Holy Spirit on me so I'm able to use my life to the praise of Your glory.

Receive the glory due Your name as I look to You with all of my heart. Receive the honor due Your name as I lift You up with honor. Let all the earth praise Your name. Let all creatures great or small adore You and offer You the glory You deserve for all You've done to create and provide for us.

CONFESSION

God, I confess that I don't always recognize the seal of the Holy Spirit as I should. You have sealed me with the Holy Spirit of promise. You've given me the Holy Spirit as a pledge of my inheritance, with a view of the redemption You offer me as Your own possession. This seal is to bring You praise and glorify You.

Yet I often go days, weeks, or even months without giving the Holy Spirit so much as a casual thought. Forgive me for falling short in this area of my life. I want to grow and become more spiritually mature, so please help me do that.

THANKSGIVING

Father, thank You for the seal of the Holy Spirit. Thank You for honoring my life and my dignity by giving me the promise of Your presence and a pledge of my inheritance in You. Thank You for not simply passing over me because there are so many people to care for in this world. You know me by name, and You recognize me as Your heir to all of the spiritual wonders and gifts You have to offer.

SUPPLICATION

Lord God, I ask that Your seal of the Holy Spirit remind me to trust in You. You've promised to take care of me if I put my hope in You, so I do that right now. Let the seal of the Holy Spirit be my connection to the eternal inheritance I have as a child of the King.

Show me how to remember this connection on a more regular basis so I can take full advantage of all of the rights and privileges You have for me. I ask for spiritual wisdom, hope, perseverance, and so much more that You offer me through this precious seal of the Holy Spirit on me.

10

The Breath

By the word of the LORD the heavens were made,
and by the breath of His mouth all their host.
PSALM 33:6

ADORATION

Father, Your Holy Spirit has the power to create. Your breath is made manifest in the Spirit, giving life to whatever You provide. When You created the world, You spoke it into being. Breath came from You to give life and vitality to all it touched. This same breath that created the world is available to me through an abiding relationship with Your Holy Spirit.

I love You and praise You for how You make yourself available to me to worship You. May Your name be praised, and may You receive the glory due You in all things.

CONFESSION

God, I confess that far too often I've taken the power of Your creation for granted. I don't stop to marvel as I should. What You've made and how You've made it through the power of Your breath, which comes forth as the Holy Spirit, is amazing. But I confess that I haven't praised

You as I should. At times, I've even taken my own life and the miracle of my own existence for granted.

Forgive me for neglecting to honor You and praise You for who You are and for the greatness that resides in the Holy Spirit, the breath of God.

THANKSGIVING

Father, thank You for loving me. Thank You for creating me. Thank You for creating the world in which I can live. Thank You for the food I'm able to eat. All of this came about through Your breath. Yet You didn't stop there. You've given me the breath of the Holy Spirit as my own, to have in me. I have access to the very breath that created the world.

Thank You for loving me enough to give me the Holy Spirit and His presence within. Thank You for quickening my spirit within so I can get to know You more through praying these prayers according to the name and power of Your Holy Spirit.

SUPPLICATION

Lord God, I ask that Your breath, the Holy Spirit, breathe in me a newness of life, wonder, and joy. I ask that the breath of the Holy Spirit renew my spiritual fervor and draw me closer to You. Show me how to honor You with my life as I come to know the breath of God, the Holy Spirit, in a more intimate manner.

Give me the wisdom I need to live my life spiritually and not just for myself. You've placed me here to glorify You in all that I do. Let me glorify You in my choices, hopes, and dreams. Let my breath produce words that glorify You and give You honor as the powerful, almighty God You are.

11

The Power

*I will not presume to speak of anything except what
Christ has accomplished through me, resulting in the
obedience of the Gentiles by word and deed, in the
power of signs and wonders, in the power of the Spirit;
so that from Jerusalem and round about as far as
Illyricum I have fully preached the gospel of Christ.*

ROMANS 15:18-19

ADORATION

Father, Your power is made manifest in the world in so many ways. I see it in Your creation. I see it in how You direct occurrences. Your power gives life, breath, and purpose.

But Your power also shows up and is accessed through a personal relationship with Your Holy Spirit. The power of the Spirit is available to me, and I praise You for making it this way. I don't have to rely on my own power. When I'm weak, You make me strong through the presence of Your Holy Spirit. I worship You because You're the great God who oversees all and provides for all.

CONFESSION

God, I confess that I don't always tap into the power of the Holy Spirit as I should. For some reason, I feel like I can make it through the tough times and troubles in this life on my own. Or maybe I just forget to call on the power of the Holy Spirit. Too many times, I also try to seek my own way in carrying out Your will.

But in Romans 15 Paul reminds me that he preached the gospel of Christ only through the power of the Holy Spirit. I need to be sure my good works are rooted and grounded in the power of the Holy Spirit too. Forgive me when I charge forward, attempting to serve You in my own strength.

THANKSGIVING

Father, thank You for the power You make available to me through the connection I have with the abiding Holy Spirit within me. I love You for so many things, and one of them is this gift of the Holy Spirit. It's Your power that enables me to serve You and share Your gospel with others.

Thank You for how You've shown me Your will and enabled me to do so many wonderful things to promote Your kingdom agenda. I know it's all because of the indwelling power of the Spirit.

SUPPLICATION

Lord God, I want to do more to bring You glory and advance Your kingdom agenda on earth. I want to glorify You in all that I do. Will You remind me to tap into the power of the Holy Spirit so that I will always rely on His strength?

Show me great spiritual success as I use the power of the Spirit in all I do. And in those times I'm weak and struggling, I ask that the power of the Holy Spirit be my strength. May the Holy Spirit support me when I need it the most and give me the focus I need to go through each day in a way that's pleasing to You.

12

The Wind

Suddenly there came from heaven
a noise like a violent rushing wind,
and it filled the whole house
where they were sitting.

ACTS 2:2

ADORATION

Father, Your creation reflects You, whether it's wind, fire, rain, snow, sleet, or anything else. You are a loving God who cares for us through what You've created. I praise You for seeing fit to minister to each of us while we're here on earth. I worship You for Your desire to provide for us to reflect Your glory. Your Holy Spirit is where we find strength and joy and peace.

But even more than that, we find the strength to live out Your calling. This comes through the fire of Your Spirit, which burns within, and the wind of Your Spirit, which motivates and propels us to move forward in the purpose and pathway You have for us to walk in.

CONFESSION

God, I confess that I try to carry out the purpose I have for my own life on my own. I want certain things, and I'd like to experience certain achievements, and so I set aside Your provision of the wind of the Spirit and press forward in my own strength.

Forgive me for neglecting the power You have for me through this wind of the Spirit. Wind is powerful. Wind can move things alone. Wind can guide things along. Forgive me for neglecting these great gifts and blessings of the Holy Spirit.

THANKSGIVING

Father, thank You for Your loving care and the hope that comes in Your name. Thank You for the provision of Your Holy Spirit. Bless me with a heart full of gratitude so I'm more able to recognize Your provision in my life.

Thank You for never giving up on me, instead always being there for me when I need You most. You're there for me through the presence of the wind of the Spirit. Your wind came to the apostles when they huddled together in fear before You called them out to take the gospel to the world. Thank You for the might and strength of Your wind in their lives, which enabled the gospel to come to me as well.

SUPPLICATION

Lord God, I ask that You reveal to me Your greatest will for my life. What is Your preferred will that I should carry out on Your behalf?

Like the apostles huddled in the upper room, I huddle now in prayer before You. I ask that You make Your will for me known and then equip me with a special wind of the Spirit, which will lift my spirit and mind to focus on what You would have me do. Keep me free from distractions Satan sends my way. Show me how I can please You and honor You in all that I do.

13

The Spirit of Wisdom

If any of you lacks wisdom, let him ask of God,
who gives to all generously and without reproach,
and it will be given to him.

JAMES 1:5

ADORATION

Father, Your offer of wisdom—which You freely give—is always on the table for Your followers. I worship You because You are the great God of all wisdom. You know all things. You understand all things. You see the end from the beginning, and You offer to help us navigate the difficulties of life.

The way to spiritual success comes through wisdom. Wisdom is like gold; it is precious. If we seek You, we seek wisdom. The closer we are to You, the closer we are to living a wise life. All of the wisdom You have within You is what makes the world function. I honor You and worship You for the wisdom it takes for the world to operate as it does, according to Your natural laws and great wisdom.

CONFESSION

God, I confess that I often stumble through life with blinders on. I'm not blind, and yet I wear these blinders when I choose to live my life without the wisdom that is free from You. I can pull off the blinders by asking You for wisdom.

Forgive me for neglecting to ask You for wisdom. Forgive me for failing to honor You by living a life of wisdom. I've made so many foolish choices and committed so many sins out of a lack of wisdom. I ask for Your loving care as You shower me with both mercy and wisdom.

THANKSGIVING

Father, thank You for the gift of the Holy Spirit, who offers me access to Your wisdom. The Holy Spirit is the Spirit of Wisdom. Within Him resides all the wisdom within You. And I thank You for making Him available to me simply when I choose to ask.

Thank You for loving me so much that You've given me the ability to tap into Your wisdom whenever I want. I don't have to pray an elaborate prayer or perform a spiritual exercise in order to gain wisdom. I just have to ask. Thank You for making the Spirit so accessible to me whenever I need or want wisdom.

SUPPLICATION

Lord God, I ask for Your wisdom to know how I can better live my life in a way that pleases and glorifies You. I also ask for Your wisdom on how to keep a closer, more abiding relationship with the Holy Spirit so I can truly gain all I need from my relationship with Him.

Show me how to say more effective prayers. Teach me the wisdom I need to pray prayers that are in alignment with Your will for my life. Give me all I need through the Holy Spirit and His wisdom so I can live victoriously as a spiritual warrior and advance Your kingdom agenda on earth.

14

The Spirit of Counsel

The Counselor, the Holy Spirit,
whom the Father will send in my name,
he will teach you all things,
and bring to your remembrance
all that I have said to you.

JOHN 14:26 RSV

ADORATION

Father, I don't need to live with a troubled heart full of anxiety and worry. You've promised me peace, and I can gain this peace through Your counsel. You provide Your counsel to me through the presence of the Holy Spirit, who is the Great Counselor. He is the Spirit of Counsel, and He offers me all I need to overcome stress, trauma, triggers, and difficulties.

I give You praise for Your loving-kindness. I honor You for Your peace. I worship You for Your counsel, available to me through the Holy Spirit. May Your name receive the glory due You, great God and ruler over all.

CONFESSION

God, I confess that far too often I sin out of foolishness, and yet You offer me counsel anytime I need it. You have sent the Holy Spirit, who came in Jesus Christ's name, and yet I neglect to take advantage of His counsel.

I ask for Your forgiveness. Forgive me for every foolish choice I made when You were there to guide me with Your Holy Spirit yet I did not ask for guidance. Forgive me for every harmful word I said to someone—or to myself through negative self-talk—when instead I could have asked the Holy Spirit for counsel. Forgive me for my sins, for they are many.

THANKSGIVING

Father, thank You for offering me the counsel I need to navigate life and become spiritually successful in all I do. Thank You for not leaving me in the dark spiritually, instead sending the Holy Spirit, who is given to me through Jesus Christ and my faith in Him.

Thank You for showing me the way when I don't know the way. You guide me through Your Word. You also counsel me through the perfect presence of Your Spirit. Thank You that when I follow Your counsel, I can live a life of peace, hope, and security.

SUPPLICATION

Lord God, I ask for Your counsel. I start by asking for counsel from the Holy Spirit on how to live more according to Your counsel. I can't live according to Your counsel when I neglect to look to the Spirit for it. So that is the first thing I ask for—greater counsel on how to live by the power of the Spirit.

Show me what I need to do differently to live by Your Spirit's counsel. Show me how to tap into the presence of Your Spirit on a regular basis. Guide me in the understanding and application of Your Word through the power of the Holy Spirit's counsel working in me.

The Spirit of Knowledge

To each one is given the manifestation of the Spirit for the common good. For to one is given the word of wisdom through the Spirit, and to another the word of knowledge according to the same Spirit.

1 CORINTHIANS 12:7-8

ADORATION

Father, Your gifts of the Spirit are a blessing to each person who receives them. Your Holy Spirit has so many wonderful, powerful, and enriching gifts to bestow upon those who follow You. Your gifts include wisdom, teaching, preaching, and knowledge, and the Spirit of Knowledge enables us to grow in the grace and knowledge of our Lord Jesus Christ.

You are a generous and benevolent God who bestows on us all we need to live as Your kingdom followers. You enable me to know You more through the gift of knowledge made manifest in Your Holy Spirit. I worship You and adore You for the gifts You've made available to me.

CONFESSION

God, I confess my lack of spiritual knowledge even though Your Holy Spirit grants me access to greater knowledge through the shed blood of Jesus Christ. I confess that I don't access this knowledge fully as I should.

Forgive me for how I've neglected the spiritual growth that's mine through an intimate relationship with You. Please also forgive me for the sins I've committed rooted in Satan's deception. Your Holy Spirit can enable me to be wise to Satan's schemes, and I ask for Your forgiveness for falling prey to Satan's trickery and deception time and time again despite all You've provided me to overcome him.

THANKSGIVING

Father, thank You for offering me knowledge through the manifestation of the Holy Spirit. You desire to bring about the greatest common good for all of humanity, and the Holy Spirit has been sent to help us access this common good and be blessed by it. We all play a part, and Your Spirit offers so many diverse gifts.

Thank You for the gift of knowledge—the word of knowledge according to the Holy Spirit. Let this word of knowledge be found by all who seek it. Thank You for making the Spirit available to all who seek Him. Thank You for bringing about good to all of us in the body of Christ through the various gifts of the Spirit You supply us. Thank You that we're together in Your church to benefit from one another.

SUPPLICATION

Lord God, I ask that You pour out the word of knowledge upon all who are blessed by this specific gift of the Holy Spirit. Pour out the mighty release of Your gifts upon all who seek You.

Help the body of Christ be enriched by all the great gifts of Your Spirit—but especially by the word of knowledge. Give us wisdom into Your Holy Word and into who You are as our Lord. Show each of us how to apply the Spirit of Knowledge's revelation in ways that help build up the church and strengthen families. Show me how to be more receptive to the gifts of the Holy Spirit in my own life.

16

The Spirit of Truth

*When He, the Spirit of truth, comes, He will guide
you into all the truth; for He will not speak on His
own initiative, but whatever He hears, He will speak;
and He will disclose to you what is to come.*

JOHN 16:13

ADORATION

Father, Your awareness of everything taking place both in the past and the future is exhaustive. You understand how all things work together according to Your plan, but we have a limited view.

Yet Your Holy Spirit was sent to disclose what You desire for us to know. I praise You for the gift of the Holy Spirit to me, a gift that enables me to gain wisdom and greater awareness of Your will and how it's carried out in the physical realm through the spiritual realm. I worship You for the complexity of who You are and yet the simplicity of the Holy Spirit in translating deep, spiritual truths to each of us who have an ear to hear.

CONFESSION

God, I confess that my fear of the future and worry about things to come often seep into my present moments and distract me from worshiping You or following You as I should. I confess that I don't always keep my eyes focused on the gifts You have for me right now because I'm concerned about things to come.

And yet the Holy Spirit can guide me into all truth so that I don't need to guess. Forgive me for neglecting to tap into the Spirit's guiding as often as I could and should.

THANKSGIVING

Father, thank You for the gift of the Holy Spirit, who is the Spirit of Truth. Thank You for sending the Holy Spirit, who can guide me into all truth. Thank You that the Holy Spirit does not speak on His own initiative. He doesn't speak contrary to Your own will. Whatever the Holy Spirit hears from You, He will speak. And whatever the Holy Spirit sees in You, He can share and disclose what is to come.

The Holy Spirit is a gift to help give me wisdom on how to avoid and escape the snares of the evil one—Satan.

SUPPLICATION

Lord God, I ask for wisdom about what is to come, as the Holy Spirit is able to disclose truth to me. I ask that I trade my worry and fear for peace in the truth of the Holy Spirit. I ask for greater strength to manifest itself in me spiritually as I gain more access to the truth of the Holy Spirit. Show me how to use the truth the Holy Spirit reveals to me in ways that bring You glory and bring other people good.

I also ask for an increased level of my own ability to speak Your truth in love through the power of the Holy Spirit in me. Make me know Your truth through drawing me into a deeper, more intimate relationship with the Holy Spirit.

The Advocate Who Testifies

When the Helper comes, whom I will send to you
from the Father, that is the Spirit of truth who
proceeds from the Father, He will testify about Me.

JOHN 15:26

ADORATION

Father, Your character and greatness exceed anything I could ever understand on my own. The Spirit who is the Advocate testifies as to who You are and Your goodness. He also testifies about Jesus Christ and the truth found in my Lord and Savior.

The Holy Spirit knows You and reveals You, but He's also my advocate to go to You on my behalf. Because the Spirit knows You and me so well, He can advocate on my behalf in ways I will never understand but will forever be grateful for. I worship You and honor You. You are beyond my understanding, and I lift Your name in praise.

CONFESSION

God, I confess that I fail to turn to the Advocate, who is the Holy Spirit, as much as I could. Too often, I instead try to figure out things on my own. Or I even wallow in guilt and shame because I've not taken the Advocate seriously.

The shed blood of Jesus Christ cleanses me from all of my sins, and only when I choose to remain in a state of guilt and shame does Satan gain another stronghold in my life. Will You please forgive me for how I've neglected this active role of the Holy Spirit, who's been sent on Your behalf to advocate for mine?

THANKSGIVING

Father, thank You for all You've done to bring me from a place of despair to a place of hope. Thank You for providing me with the Holy Spirit, whose many gifts set me free in the truth and knowledge of the Lord Jesus Christ. Thank You that the Advocate testifies of who You are and who Christ is and can also testify to You on my behalf as I seek restoration and spiritual healing.

You know my form and that I am but dust, so I trust that the Holy Spirit will seek my good and Your glory in all things, allowing me to experience mercy and grace in my times of need.

SUPPLICATION

Lord God, I ask that the Holy Spirit advocate on my behalf in ways and areas I don't even know to ask. Please enact the Holy Spirit's role as Advocate on my behalf in full force. Let me experience the freeing love of the Spirit as I look to You for my full and abundant life in Christ Jesus.

I don't have to hide or be ashamed, because I can trust in the Lord Jesus Christ for all that I need, including the forgiveness of my sins. Let the Advocate stand strong before You, testifying that I desire to live a life pleasing to You and that I'm seeking how to do so.

18

The Spirit of God

The earth was formless and void,
and darkness was over the surface of the deep,
and the Spirit of God was moving
over the surface of the waters.

GENESIS 1:2

ADORATION

Father, Your Holy Spirit is the Spirit of God. Your Holy Spirit is You and reflects You in ways that help me know You better. Although I can't understand all of the details of who You are and how You're manifest through God, Christ, and the Spirit, I know I benefit from knowing You in all of these forms.

The world was created through You, and it was the Spirit of God who moved over the surface of the waters to create the earth on which we live. I worship You for Your creative strength, wisdom, and power. You've made things so beautifully intricate for me to enjoy. Thank You for the Spirit of God through whom You manifest Your glory.

CONFESSION

God, I confess that I don't understand how You're made manifest through the various Persons of the Trinity. And I don't always know how to interact with You or engage with You. I confess that some things leave me with questions because they're mysterious.

So I ask that You forgive me for pulling back from You when I'm confused or don't know what to say to You or how to speak to You. Forgive me for not pursuing knowing You as much as I should and could.

THANKSGIVING

Father, thank You for the Spirit of God, through whom You created the world I enjoy so much. Thank You for the trees and the sky and the water and the creatures You've placed on the earth. You've given so much thought to the world You made, and I know You've given thought to me too.

I love You and thank You for making me so beautifully intricate. You hold me together in Your great and mighty hand. I worship You and thank You for helping me see and be grateful for all You've done both in me and through me for Your great name and to advance Your rule on earth.

SUPPLICATION

Lord God, I ask for Your help in discerning what Your will is for me. Will You allow the Spirit of God to guide me and form my thoughts like You used Him to form the earth and all things?

Show me how I'm to walk to make the most of my days, benefit others, and bring good to all around me. Honor me with Your love and care, and give me Your grace as I seek to live out Your will in me. Show me what is my highest good so that I can gain wisdom from the Spirit of God, who makes manifest Your will in my life.

19

The Dweller in the Temple

*Do you not know that you are a temple of God
and that the Spirit of God dwells in you?*
1 CORINTHIANS 3:16

ADORATION

Father, I am a temple for You, and Your Spirit dwells in me. That truth makes me realize how much You must really love me.

The fact that You want to be close to me helps me feel Your love for me. You ask me to abide in Jesus Christ, and I do. But You also abide in me, making my body and my life Your temple, where You choose to hang out. I worship You and praise You for how great You are, yet in Your greatness, You choose to be close to me.

CONFESSION

God, I confess that I don't always make for a great temple. I examine my thoughts and wonder what You must think as You make Your home in my life.

Lord, forgive me for the wrong thoughts and sinful desires I act on and carry out. Forgive me for neglecting to maintain a pure and holy temple for Your Spirit to make His home in. Please send me Your loving forgiveness as I confess my sin of an unclean temple because of the thoughts and actions I've known and carried out.

THANKSGIVING

Father, thank You for Your love that lets me know You value and cherish me. Thank You for making my life the temple of the Holy Spirit. Your Holy Spirit ministers to me as I open my heart to Him. Thank You for letting me experience You so closely through this experience as the temple of God with the Spirit of God dwelling in me.

Thank You that I can reflect You to those with whom I come into contact in order to bring Your love and Your values to a world in need. I thank You and praise You for Your Word, which guides me on how I should live so that my temple is a good place for Your Spirit to dwell.

SUPPLICATION

Lord God, I ask for Your great grace and mercy to cover my sins entirely and create in me a pure heart so that my life is pleasing to You. As Your Spirit dwells in me, let me know Him more intimately than ever before.

Show me how to engage the Spirit of God dwelling within me in an effective and relational way. Teach me how to speak to the Spirit of God within me as well as how to hear from Him so that I can learn, grow, and develop as a kingdom follower of Jesus Christ. Help my life reflect Your love to others at a greater level, and give me the peace that passes understanding as I navigate difficulties and storms. This way I can remain more open to hearing the Spirit of God inside of me, and I can display Your grace to those around me too.

20

The Spirit of the Sovereign Lord

*The Spirit of the Lord G*OD *is upon me, because the*
L*ORD has anointed me to bring good news to the*
afflicted; He has sent me to bind up the brokenhearted,
to proclaim liberty to captives and freedom to prisoners.

ISAIAH 61:1

ADORATION

Father, Your Word is life to my soul. Your Word brings truth to my understanding. Without Your Word, I am lost. Without the truth of Your Word, I lose hope. Thank You for Your Word.

I worship You and praise You for revealing the Spirit of the Sovereign Lord to me through Your Word. The Spirit of the Sovereign Lord came to bring good news to the afflicted. The Spirit of the Sovereign Lord was sent to bind up the brokenhearted. The Spirit of the Sovereign Lord proclaims liberty to captives and freedom to prisoners. I worship You for the purpose You've bestowed upon the Spirit of the Sovereign Lord in order to set me free from pain, guilt, and the effects of sin in this world and in my life.

CONFESSION

God, I confess that for far too long I've lived bound because I've neglected to hear and apply Your Word in my life. I regret the wasted days, weeks, and even months I've lived without the light of Your truth shining brightly over me and setting my spirit free to enjoy and embrace all You have for me.

Forgive me for having little faith. Forgive me for neglecting to explore Your Word more fully. In Your Word is where I find the Spirit of the Sovereign Lord, who's come to let me know that I'm free from shame, sin, and fear. I worship You for Your great power, grace, and forgiveness.

THANKSGIVING

Father, thank You for the Spirit of the Sovereign Lord and for sending Him to set me free from captivity. When Your Holy Spirit brings me good news of Your Word, it lifts my heart.

Thank You for lifting my heart and filling me with praise and worship for You. Thank You for not leaving me in the depths of pain or despair. Thank You for the gift of the Holy Spirit, who brings great comfort in times of need and binds up my broken heart so that I can smile, laugh, and enjoy life again. Jesus came that I might have life and have it abundantly, so I thank You for the Holy Spirit, who makes this truth available to me when He reveals the precious promises found in Your Word.

SUPPLICATION

Lord God, I ask for healing. I ask that You bind up my broken heart and help it to feel love, life, and laughter again. Set me free from the pain of my sinful decisions and regrets. Set me free from the consequences of this world and the atmospheric sin it contains.

Heal my spirit so that my faith can be strong. Heal my hope so that I can walk in newness of life, reveling in the joy You make available to me through the Spirit of the Sovereign Lord. Set a light on my path so that I can walk according to the perfect will You have for me. Show me which way I need to turn, to the right or to the left, guiding me with the wisdom of the Spirit of the Sovereign Lord.

21

The Spirit of Supplication

I will pour out on the house of David and on the inhabitants
of Jerusalem, the Spirit of grace and of supplication, so that
they will look on Me whom they have pierced; and they will
mourn for Him, as one mourns for an only son, and they will
weep bitterly over Him like the bitter weeping over a firstborn.
ZECHARIAH 12:10

ADORATION

Father, You've thought of everything we need while we navigate this life on earth. You've poured out the Spirit of Supplication so that I can look to You, Lord Jesus, and clearly see the sacrifice You made for me on the cross. This Spirit of Supplication enables me to recognize the depth of this sacrifice for my sins so that I can truly worship You according to the worship due Your name.

I praise You, my Lord and Savior, for giving Your life so that I can be set free from the consequences and pain of a life in eternity apart from the presence of God. Receive the glory due Your name for all You've done for me and provided for me through Your lifeblood. You gave Yourself as a ransom for all, so that those who believe in You can be saved through faith in You.

CONFESSION

God, I confess my lack before You. I confess my inability to preserve my soul and save myself from sin. Only through the shed blood of Jesus Christ, who gave Himself up for me on the cross and was later resurrected from the dead, do I find the peace and perfection of salvation.

Forgive me for my sins. Forgive me for neglecting to cherish my salvation as I ought. Have mercy on me, a sinner who's been saved by grace through faith in Jesus Christ. Make Your name great throughout the globe, Lord, so that others may see You and call upon You to be saved.

THANKSGIVING

Father, thank You for Your love to me, a sinner, in giving to me Jesus Christ, who died on the cross for my sins. Thank You for the sacrifice of the perfect Son of God.

Thank You that I don't have to fear pain or death because You've removed the sting of death through the sacrifice of Jesus. Thank You for all You've done and continue to do for me as I look to You with great hope in my heart. I love You and praise You for the Spirit of Supplication, given to me as a gift to open my heart and mind in order to truly reflect on and be grateful for the salvation that comes through the sacrifice of my Lord Jesus Christ.

SUPPLICATION

Lord God, I ask for a greater grace as I go through life. This greater grace will soften my heart so I will have a true understanding of what the sacrifice of Jesus Christ has done for me. Will You bless me with the Holy Spirit's presence on such a deep level that I will understand the power of the salvation that's mine in Jesus' name?

As I go about my days, make me an instrument of Your love by my sharing the gospel of Jesus with those around me. I ask that Your name be made known to those who don't yet know You. I ask that Jesus be exalted in the hearts of those yet to know Him as well. Help me spread the gospel as I honor and worship You with my life out of a heart of gratitude and hope found in Jesus' love and made manifest in me through the Spirit of Supplication.

22

The Spirit of Grace

*How much severer punishment do you think
he will deserve who has trampled under foot
the Son of God, and has regarded as unclean
the blood of the covenant by which he was
sanctified, and has insulted the Spirit of grace?*

HEBREWS 10:29

ADORATION

Father, Your grace offers salvation from the penalty of our sins. You bless each of us with the gift of eternal life when we look to You through faith alone in Christ alone. I praise You, and I give You honor for the glory due Your name. Your glory surrounds You with majesty. Your glory magnifies Your name throughout the world.

Show me Your glory, Lord, so I won't diminish the salvation You've given me in my soul and thus insult the Spirit of Grace. Help me recognize how significant the gift of salvation is so that I can truly honor You with my heart, thoughts, words, and actions.

CONFESSION

God, I confess that I've trampled underfoot the Son of God through my thoughts and disregard of the power of grace. When I've turned my back on You through sinful indulgences and other forms of dishonor to You, I've regarded as unclean the blood of the covenant.

Forgive me for failing to keep Your Word and obedience to it at the forefront of my heart and mind, thus diminishing the importance of honoring You with my life and actions. Help me know that I'm forgiven and cleansed. Give me a sign of Your forgiving power and Spirit of Grace in my life so that I can walk confidently in Your love and care.

THANKSGIVING

Father, thank You for the Spirit of Grace, who reminds me to take Your grace seriously and to lift Your name in praise through my words and actions.

Thank You that even though I've stumbled and sinned against You, You've lifted me with the Spirit of Grace, making me whole and pure again. Thank You for the opportunity to come to You for forgiveness of my sins, even the sins I've committed against You. Show me how to live a life of gratitude and honor so that You'll recognize my thanksgiving in all that I do and say.

SUPPLICATION

Lord God, I ask for a greater grace to be made manifest in my heart and mind. Give me a greater level of understanding so that I will know You more. I want to honor You with my love and actions.

Help me to never trample underfoot the sacrifice Jesus made on my behalf, giving me the free gift of salvation so that I can spend eternity with You. Walk with me not only in the cool of the day but during my greatest moments of anguish in life's storms. Let me know Your presence so that I'm sensitive to the holy Spirit of Grace and His work in my life, giving me both the motivation and power to live a life that's pleasing to You in all that I do in Your name and for Your glory.

23

The Spirit of Holiness

*[Jesus], who was declared the Son of God
with power by the resurrection from the
dead, according to the Spirit of holiness.*

ROMANS 1:4

ADORATION

Father, Your power is made known to us through so many ways. It's revealed through Your creation. It's revealed through Your relationship with humanity. Your power is also revealed through the resurrection from the dead, which You bestowed upon Jesus Christ after His sacrifice on the cross for the forgiveness of our sins. Your Spirit of Holiness declares this power boldly so that we can all truly know who You are and how much You love us.

You've given us such grace and joy through the gift of eternal life. You've taken away fears and doubts through the presence of the Spirit of Holiness. I worship You and give You the praise due Your name for Your greatness.

CONFESSION

God, I confess my inability to live up to the standard of holiness established by Your perfection as the great and holy God. I'm unable to live a completely blameless and holy life, but Your grace and mercy satisfy me when I realize I can never be truly holy as You are.

Forgive me for those times when I fall short. Forgive my wandering heart and mind. Show me what it means to walk boldly in Your grace and forgiveness and to let the Spirit of Holiness reside in me through the shed blood of Jesus Christ. Testify to Your goodness and Your grace in my life.

THANKSGIVING

Father, thank You for honoring me with the Spirit of Holiness, who testifies to the Son of God with power by the resurrection from the dead. Thank You that Your Spirit of Holiness can come so close to me because of what Jesus did to forgive me of my sins and make my sin no longer a divider between You and me.

Thank You that Your Spirit of Holiness is like a gentle dove and testifies to me of the beauty You've made available to me as I seek You in all things. Right now, I lift to You a heart of gratitude. Let the words of my mouth and the thoughts in my mind please You, as they come from a place of gratefulness for the Spirit of Holiness, who testifies of Your holiness to me.

SUPPLICATION

Lord God, I ask for a greater level of spiritual maturity, growth, and holiness. Let the Spirit of Holiness create in me the opportunity for more love, more grace, and more kindness to those around me. I want to live a holy life in such a way that's pleasing to You in all things. Through Your Holy Spirit, I want to know You on a level I've never experienced or known due to the sin remaining in me.

Let me be cleansed and wiped clean by the Spirit of Holiness, who declares the living Lord Jesus Christ through the resurrection of the dead.

Let my spirit reflect Your Spirit in such a way that others are touched and can see Your love in me. I want to be a testimony of Jesus Christ to those around me so that they, too, can access the life-giving, saving power Jesus has given to all who place faith in Him for their salvation.

24

The Spirit of Christ

You are not in the flesh but in the Spirit,
if indeed the Spirit of God dwells in you.
But if anyone does not have the Spirit of Christ,
he does not belong to Him.

ROMANS 8:9

ADORATION

Father, Your willingness to draw close to me so I can belong to You through the Spirit of Christ gives me great comfort and peace. I lift Your name in praise and adoration, knowing that You cause all things to work together for good according to Your perfect will and for those who love You and are called according to Your purpose. I honor You for how You're working in my own heart to develop and mature me into a kingdom disciple.

Receive my praise and take delight as I worship You, my Lord. Make me into a living vessel of praise to You.

CONFESSION

God, I confess that I often go about my own thoughts or ways without remembering that I belong to You. It's a gift to belong to You. I have the Spirit of Christ in me because I've trusted in Jesus Christ for salvation from my sins.

Forgive me for forgetting that I belong to You and then making my own decisions apart from turning to You for Your wisdom and guidance. Please have mercy on me, as I am a sinner and in need of Your forgiveness and love. I belong to You, so I want to honor You with all that I am and all that I do.

THANKSGIVING

Father, thank You that I belong to You because of the Spirit of Christ, who lives in me. Thank You for loving me so much that You saw the distance between us and bridged it by sending Your Son, Jesus Christ, who died on the cross so that I could be fully forgiven and made perfect and complete in You.

Thank You for all the precious promises and gifts that come to me through the indwelling of the Holy Spirit. And thank You for loving me enough to not give up on me but to continue to help me grow and learn through life's challenges as well as through studying Your Holy Word.

SUPPLICATION

Lord God, I ask that the Spirit of Christ, who is in me, help me understand and discern Your Holy Word on a greater level. Show me how I can grow and develop into a kingdom disciple who reveals Your loving care to those around me. Let the Spirit of Christ in me bring me hope, peace, and joy so that I can radiate these qualities of the Spirit to those around me.

I want to be used by You, Lord—to help others know who You are and to worship You and find peace in You. Give me strength to focus on what matters most instead of getting side-tracked on what's sent as a distraction.

25

The Spirit Who Guides Our Way

*That the requirement of the Law might be fulfilled in us,
who do not walk according to the flesh
but according to the Spirit.*

ROMANS 8:4

ADORATION

Father, Your guidance is critical for me to accomplish the will You have for my life. If I'm left to my own, I can stray or divert from the path that will bring You the greatest glory and others the greatest good. But it's my desire to glorify You with my heart, thoughts, and actions. Receive the praise of my mouth as my words lift You up in honor and worship.

You've made all things, so You know how things should go. You know the end from the beginning, and it's always best for me to follow Your leading through the guidance of the Holy Spirit. I'm able to follow You when I no longer walk according to the flesh but according to the Spirit.

CONFESSION

God, I confess that I often walk according to the flesh and not according to the Spirit. This has led me down the wrong path far too many times, and it's brought me into a life of consequences I wish I didn't have to bear.

Forgive me for thinking I know more than Your Holy Spirit. Forgive me for failing to heed Your Spirit's guidance, instead turning to my flesh to show me which way to go. You are a great and mighty God, and You give guidance and direction out of a heart of love, not to confine me but to bless me. Let Your mercy be showered upon me as I look to You for my peace.

THANKSGIVING

Father, thank You for guiding me. Thank You for giving me the gift of the Holy Spirit, who makes me know Your ways and showers me with wisdom. When I walk according to the flesh, I go astray. But when I walk according to the Spirit, whom You've given to me, doors open to me so that I know which way to go.

You are the great and holy God who gives me direction through the Holy Spirit. Thank You for fulfilling the requirement of the Law in me as I walk according to the Holy Spirit.

SUPPLICATION

Lord God, I ask for Your favor as I live my life. Will you help me fulfill the requirements of the Law by my living according to Your truth?

Show me how to walk not as my flesh would have me walk but as Your Spirit shows me. Help me recognize the Holy Spirit in all that I do so that I can reflect Him in my words and actions. Show me Your love on a greater level by drawing my heart and spirit into an intimate and abiding relationship with the Holy Spirit, who guides my walking and my ways. I love You and ask that Your love lead me according to Your wise path.

26

The Spirit of Glory

If you are reviled for the name of Christ, you are blessed,
because the Spirit of glory and of God rests on you.
1 PETER 4:14

ADORATION

Father, You've allowed Yourself to experience so much in an effort to love and nourish us as Your creation. You've enabled Yourself to come to earth in the form of a servant, Jesus Christ, who then gave His life so that there could be a way for us to inherit eternal life. Those of us who trust in the Lord Jesus Christ alone in faith alone are given the gift of salvation. Yet when Jesus walked the earth, He was reviled and shunned by many.

As kingdom followers of His, we're also shunned and reviled at times. This is when I take comfort in knowing Your love at an even deeper level. I worship You, because You make Yourself known to me in the midst of my sufferings.

CONFESSION

God, I confess that I don't always stand up under reviling or persecution in a way that honors You. In fact, I tend to seek to avoid it. I've made Your glory my pursuit, but when times get tough, I sometimes turn elsewhere to avoid the pain. I pursue a life of acceptance, comfort, and peace.

Forgive me for those times I haven't stood under persecution in a way that honors You. Forgive me for when I've closed my mouth when I should have opened it in defense of the gospel and for the sake of Your glory.

THANKSGIVING

Father, thank You for loving me and giving me the blessed presence of the Holy Spirit. This Spirit of Glory and of You rests on me and brings me continual comfort and delight. Thank You that the Holy Spirit is available to me at any moment throughout the day and night.

Holy Spirit, You've given me so many gifts that I can't even begin to list them all. Make Yourself at home in my heart so that God's glory can rest fully on me as I seek to live a life punctuated by peace and gratitude.

SUPPLICATION

Lord God, I ask for Your glory to rest on me. Make me a reflection of Your love, goodness, and glory so that wherever I go, people see You in me. My prayer is to make Your name known and to expand Your glory to the furthest reaches of the earth. I ask for Your strength to do this so that my life brings You great joy and satisfaction.

When Your Holy Spirit makes His home in my heart, I'm able to draw closer to You in all ways. I ask for wisdom on how to draw closer to the Spirit so that I can remove whatever is keeping me from the full, abiding presence of the Spirit made manifest both in me and through me to others. Fill me with the Holy Spirit every moment.

The Spirit of Revelation

*That the God of our Lord Jesus Christ, the Father
of glory, may give to you a spirit of wisdom
and of revelation in the knowledge of Him.*

EPHESIANS 1:17

ADORATION

Father, Your truth is absolute. Your power is supreme. You reign above all, and Your knowledge covers all. What You reveal is what You choose to reveal, and You do this through the Holy Spirit.

I worship You, for great is Your understanding and wisdom. There is no topic about which You're unsure. If I question anything at all, I know I can find the answer in You. You are full of love and greatness, and I honor You with all of my heart.

CONFESSION

God, Your glory causes me to seek You. And yet I confess that I often try to discover the answers to my questions on my own. What confuses me can lead me down a rabbit hole of discovery, looking into things that end up confusing me even more.

Only through the revelation of the Holy Spirit can I gain access to the wisdom from above. Forgive me when I seek my own glory through a search for answers on my own. I've wasted so much of my life trying to find truth when truth is available to me through the revelation of the Holy Spirit, who has within Him the knowledge of the living Lord.

THANKSGIVING

Father, thank You for allowing me to access the truth that is Your knowledge through the Holy Spirit. Thank You that the God of our Lord Jesus Christ, the Father of glory, can give me a spirit of wisdom and of revelation in the knowledge of who You are.

Your wisdom is a gift to me, and I cherish it. Show me how I can gain even greater wisdom as I seek You every moment of each day. Fill my heart and mind with an even greater level of gratitude so that You're fully known to me as much as You'll allow Yourself to be known through the presence of the Holy Spirit in me.

SUPPLICATION

Lord God, I ask for great wisdom. I ask to know things I don't yet know. I ask that You guide me into a deeper level of truth and understanding so that I can live a life honoring to You and Your glory. I want to advance Your kingdom agenda on earth. I want to live as a kingdom follower of Jesus Christ. But I need a greater allowance of Your great wisdom to do this.

Shower Your wisdom on me through the expression of the Holy Spirit in me so that I'm full of the knowledge of the God who made everything and knows everything. I ask for Your Holy Spirit to quicken in me a greater desire for wisdom and truth so that I can be filled with even more revelation You have for me to explore and apply.

28

The Spirit of Adoption

You have not received a spirit of
slavery leading to fear again,
but you have received a spirit of adoption as sons
by which we cry out, "Abba! Father!"

ROMANS 8:15

ADORATION

Father, Your love extends further than I could ever imagine. You love me so much that You were willing to adopt me into Your family. You've brought me close to You in ways I never imagined. Your glory sits outside of my understanding, and You've chosen to give me the Holy Spirit, causing me to call You Father.

I love You and adore You. I lift Your name in praise and honor. Receive the glory due You as the Holy Spirit gathers Your family around You to bring You glory in all things.

CONFESSION

God, I confess that sometimes I forget that I can call You Father. I forget that You've chosen to make me an heir of Your kingdom according to the righteousness of the Lord Jesus Christ.

Forgive me for living as an orphan when I'm not an orphan. Forgive me for living as unloved when I'm wholly loved by You. Make Your mercy mine not only in experience but as a way of life so that I walk in Your forgiveness, strengthened by Your closeness to me as my loving Father.

THANKSGIVING

Father, thank You, for I have not received a spirit of slavery leading to fear again. Rather, I've received a spirit of adoption as Your child, by which I cry out to You by name. You are my Father, and that tells me how much You love me. Thank You for bringing me into the safety of Your covering as my loving Father. Thank You for honoring me with Your presence and the gift of the Holy Spirit.

Thank You, Holy Spirit, for being the instrument through which I gain access to God's family. I am an heir and fully loved as a family member.

SUPPLICATION

Lord God, reveal to me all of the benefits that come from being Your child in the family of the Lord Jesus Christ, my Savior. Help me maximize these benefits in my life and make the most of my standing through the Holy Spirit and my adoption into Your kingdom family. Show me my inheritance both now and for eternity so that I will gain greater insight into and motivation for serving You with all of my heart. I belong to You, God, through the adoption of the Holy Spirit. Show me Your great grace as I live in the revelation of what this adoption truly means.

Holy Spirit, reveal to me the value I have as a legitimate child of the King of kings. I no longer have to find my own way or lend myself to my own understanding. I now know I'm a loved family member.

29

The Spirit of Faith

Having the same spirit of faith,
according to what is written,
"I believed, therefore I spoke," we also
believe, therefore we also speak.

2 CORINTHIANS 4:13

ADORATION

Father, Your Word is a lamp unto my feet. Your Word guides me and guards me. I find safety in the truth in Your Word. Your Word tells me I live with the holy Spirit of Faith in me as Your child. The faith that is the Holy Spirit's is available to me.

You've given me this gift to increase my faith when I'm lacking in faith. The Scripture says, "We also believe, therefore we also speak," and I, too, want to believe in You and Your Word and thus speak what is pleasing to You in all things. I want my words to glorify and lift You up so that You truly know the fullness of my adoration for You, my great King and Lord.

CONFESSION

God, I confess that I have great faith on what's easy, but I'm weak when my faith is tested. I admit this and ask for Your forgiveness. Let the Spirit of Faith fill me with a greater level of faith so that I will live in a way that honors You and brings good to me through that which is accomplished only through faith.

My belief in You and Your Word isn't always what it should or could be, so I ask that Your forgiveness cover me and keep me from the evil one so that I'm not drawn into an even lower level of faith or higher level of doubt or apathy.

THANKSGIVING

Father, thank You for faith. Thank You for setting up Your kingdom in such a way that You reward faith. Faith is Your love language, and You've given me the Spirit of Faith so I can carry out acts of faith in Your name. I thank You for letting me honor and serve You through my beliefs. I believe Your Word, and I believe the promises in Your Word, which You've made available to me.

Thank You, Holy Spirit, for feeding my faith with the Spirit of Faith so it can grow and magnify God's great plan on earth.

SUPPLICATION

Lord God, I ask for the Holy Spirit to develop in me a greater level of faith. I want a faith that's assured. I want a faith that's solid. I want the faith of the heroes I read about in the book of Hebrews. Shower me with the Spirit of Faith to such a degree that my faith can't help but grow and blossom into everything it should be.

I want to perform acts of service to others that honor You, but I want to do it with a heart of love and faith. Increase both in me so that I can bring joy to those around me. Show me the rewards of faith both in the present life and in the eternal life to come. Will you grace me with a deeper awareness of You and the Holy Spirit's abiding in me so that I can tap into the inexhaustible faith given to fuel me?

30

The Eternal Spirit

How much more will the blood of Christ,
who through the eternal Spirit offered Himself
without blemish to God,
cleanse your conscience from dead
works to serve the living God?

HEBREWS 9:14

ADORATION

Father, You've offered me eternal life through the shed blood of Jesus Christ. You've given me the forgiveness of my sins because I've placed my faith alone in Christ alone. What's more, You've allowed my conscience to be cleansed from dead works so that I can serve You, the living God, because of the Eternal Spirit, who has offered Himself without blemish to You.

The gift of the Eternal Spirit is priceless. It frees me up to live a life of service, joy, peace, and dedication to You. The shed blood of Christ cleansed me from all of my sins. The Eternal Spirit cleansed my conscience from dead works that produced nothing. Only Your love can produce good works through me, and I praise You for enabling me to understand this so that I can worship You as You so deserve.

CONFESSION

God, I confess that I've spent too much of my life focused on dead works—works done out of the power of my flesh and even to my own glory. They may look like good works to others, but You know the heart. You know my conscience. You know I need the Eternal Spirit to cleanse me from these dead works so that I can serve You with a heart of authenticity and love.

Forgive me for patting my own back. Forgive me for online posting about the good works I do, seeking to draw attention to myself. Give me the grace I need to truly serve You according to the power given me through the shed blood of Jesus Christ and the gift of life made manifest in me in the Eternal Spirit.

THANKSGIVING

Father, thank You for the cleansing of my conscience from dead works, which amount to nothing. Apart from You, I can do nothing. Shower me with Your love as I lift my heart in gratitude to You. You are worthy to be thanked and to receive the gratefulness in my heart as I lift up this prayer to You.

Let this prayer, therefore, please You. It comes from a spirit of thanksgiving, made alive through the Eternal Spirit, who's cleansed me of the desire to carry out my righteousness in my own strength. True righteousness and good works are rooted in the blood and saving power of the Lord Jesus Christ.

SUPPLICATION

Lord God, I ask You to set me free through the cleansing power of the Eternal Spirit in me, to perform great works in Your name. I want to take the gospel to this world that needs to hear it. I want to honor You with my life and choices.

My conscience has been made clean, so now I ask You to use my life to glorify You with good works founded on You in all ways. Bless me with the Eternal Spirit, who gives me all I need to live alive and clean before You. Bless me through the blood of Jesus, who gave Himself as a ransom so that I may be released from the bondage of sin and pride and set apart to carry out the good works that will truly glorify You.

31

The Spirit of Renewal

You send forth Your Spirit, they are created;
and You renew the face of the ground.

PSALM 104:30

ADORATION

Father, Your renewal is a blessing that comes down from heaven. You renew the grass with the blessing of rain. You renew our health with the blessing of sunshine. You also renew hope with the blessing of Your Word. You are the source and provider of renewal in so many ways.

It's easy to forget all that and just come to expect that all things renew automatically. But any drought reminds us they do not. Any sickness immediately reminds us they do not. You are the supplier of renewal, and You do this through Your Holy Spirit, whom You've sent to bless us and renew us with His refreshing presence and love.

CONFESSION

God, I confess that I remain weary longer than I should or need to because I forget to go to the Holy Spirit to be refreshed. I'm so easily distracted. Forgive me for failing to pay attention to something as important as this. The Spirit of Renewal is available to me whenever I want to access Your renewing presence and power.

Show me how to honor You through living in awareness of the Spirit of Renewal so that I will fulfill my purpose, strengthened in You.

THANKSGIVING

Father, thank You for the Spirit of Renewal. Thank You for sending forth Your Spirit and creating everything You desire. Thank You for sending forth Your Spirit and renewing the face of the ground. You give life to the vegetation. You give life to the animals. You give life to humanity. You renew this earth moment by moment so that we are not extinguished.

Thank You for Your love made manifest through this Spirit of Renewal. Thank You for loving us so much that You don't leave us to want or wander on our own. You make Yourself known to us through Your precious Holy Spirit.

SUPPLICATION

Lord God, I ask for renewal. I ask to be refreshed. I ask that my spiritual life and spiritual focus be made new through the abiding presence of the holy Spirit of Renewal. As You renew the grass and the ground, renew my spirit in me. As You renew the vegetation and animals, renew my mind and thoughts.

Give me fresh eyes to read Your Word and understand it. Give me a fresh heart to feel and experience Your love. Make my feet renewed so I can walk in the Spirit and carry out the good works You've established for me to do. Show me all I need to do to seek Your face and find the Spirit of Renewal, available to me now. With Your renewal, I'll have the power and wisdom to leave a lasting kingdom impact on all those around me, and I will bring You great joy.

32

The Spirit of Judgment and Burning

When the Lord has washed away the filth of the daughters of Zion and purged the bloodshed of Jerusalem from her midst, by the spirit of judgment and the spirit of burning...

ISAIAH 4:4

ADORATION

Father, Your wrath doesn't go unnoticed. Throughout time, You've poured out Your wrath on those who sinned against You. This is inescapable apart from the shed blood of Jesus Christ. Your Holy Spirit not only brings goodness and spiritual power upon the earth but is an instrument of Your judgment and burning anger against unrighteousness. Your Holy Spirit carries out the burning and destruction in Your name so that people will know You are the holy God and that there is no one apart from You.

I worship You, for You are holy, pure, and just in all You do. You carry out the punishment of evil so that evil will grasp its limits. You seek to instruct us in the way of wisdom. And our learning through Your wrath is one way You do this, so I praise Your name for Your loving care, which has given us the Spirit of Judgment and Burning to reveal Your displeasure against sin.

CONFESSION

God, I confess my sins before You. I ask for the forgiveness I need to cleanse me from all of my unrighteousness. Forgive me for neglecting You as first priority in my life. You are holy, and I am not. But because I trust in the Lord Jesus Christ for the forgiveness of my sins, I can be spared Your wrath.

Show me great mercy and spare me from the Spirit of Judgment and Burning that has been dealt upon so many. Help me experience what it means to live forgiven. I want to walk in the fullness of joy that comes from knowing Your love. Your mercy has been showered upon me with great care and grace.

THANKSGIVING

Father, thank You for Your forgiveness of my sins. Thank You for my knowing that I am dust and that You formed humanity from the dust of the ground. Thank You for holding back the full wrath due me as a result of my pride, sin, and indolence. Show me what it means to fully serve You and live a life pleasing to You.

As I lift my spirit in gratitude and thanksgiving for the salvation shown me through Jesus Christ, I ask that Your Spirit of Judgment and Burning find no place upon me. Instead, let me spend my days thanking You for who You are and for the love You've given me through forgiving me and teaching me how to follow You more fully.

SUPPLICATION

Lord God, I ask that You bring forgiveness to those who need to experience it. I ask that the love of Jesus Christ will compel those who are not saved that they may be saved. Send out missionaries to take the gospel of Jesus to those who haven't yet heard that they may be spared the punishment for their sins.

Lord, You've given the way to eternal life through Jesus, so I ask that You help me make Him known through my life and work in all I do and say.

33

The Spirit Who Searches the Depths of God

To us God revealed them through the Spirit;
for the Spirit searches all things, even the depths of God.
1 CORINTHIANS 2:10

ADORATION

Father, Your depths reach beyond what any human could ever know, for the depths of God are unsearchable. And yet the Holy Spirit is able to search all things. The Holy Spirit is able to search even the depths of God. And this same Holy Spirit is available to me through my abiding relationship with Jesus Christ.

I worship You for making Yourself known and available to me because of the gift of the Holy Spirit, who searches all things. The Holy Spirit's knowledge is endless, because His knowledge is Your knowledge. The Holy Spirit reveals to me what I need to know, and I worship You because of this great gift of intimacy with You.

CONFESSION

God, I confess my lack of awareness of all You truly are. And yet I have access to the Holy Spirit, who reveals You to me and searches all things, even the depths of You.

Holy Spirit, I confess that I fail to ask You all of the questions I have about the Father. Instead, I try to figure out God on my own. All the while, You patiently wait, ready to reveal Him to me in a way I could never discover on my own. I confess that I'm inadequate in my knowledge of the depths of God. Forgive me for failing to ponder and seek as I should. Convict me in a way that will draw me closer to You and closer to knowing and loving the Lord God of heaven and earth.

THANKSGIVING

Father, thank You for giving me the gift of the Holy Spirit, who is full of all knowledge and wisdom. Thank You for not hiding Yourself from me, Your child. You've made Yourself known through the Spirit. You've opened up Yourself and who You are so that I can benefit from knowing You. Thank You for loving me so much that You give me the power of the Holy Spirit within me to show me all I'm lacking. I, too, want to search Your depths through a greater awareness given to me by the Holy Spirit.

Thank You for all You've shown me, Holy Spirit, and all You will show me as I focus my heart and my mind on You.

SUPPLICATION

Lord God, I ask to know You. I ask to feel You in a way that understands Your heart, mind, and desires. Show me what makes You happy so that I can pursue what that is with fervor. Show me what makes You sad so I can avoid those things. Draw me close to You, Lord, through the Holy Spirit, who searches all things, even Your very depths. In the Holy Spirit I find all I need to honor You through fulfilling my purpose.

As I draw close to You, Holy Spirit, who searches the depths of God, I draw close to God and come to understand who I am and what He's made me to live out as my destiny in Him.

34

The Spirit of Justice

A spirit of justice for him who sits in judgment,
a strength to those who repel the onslaught at the gate.
ISAIAH 28:6

ADORATION

Father, Your justice goes before You and announces Your greatness and holiness. You are a mighty and just God. You are holy and complete. The Holy Spirit represents You as a Spirit of Justice bringing justice to the land. The Holy Spirit carries out Your justice for You, Lord.

The Holy Spirit of Justice lifts the needy and levels the proud. You are a righteous God who has authority to do whatever You want in Your kingdom, and yet You rule with love. You rule with peace. You rule with justice. You are kind and gracious, and the Holy Spirit of Justice reflects this to us. It's good that You bring justice, or all chaos would ensue. The Spirit of Justice reminds us to honor You with a heart of purity and devotion.

CONFESSION

God, I confess that I've neglected to recognize Your holiness as I should. I've neglected to show You the honor You're due. Forgive me for elevating my own self in my eyes, even above You. You sit in judgment on those who live in sin.

And yet because of the shed blood of Jesus Christ, I'm saved from Your wrath. The Spirit of Justice doesn't deal a harsh blow to me as I deserve. Rather, He offers me a justice of grace and peace. I thank You for the great forgiveness You've given me.

THANKSGIVING

Thank You, Holy Spirit, for loving me. Thank You for serving as a mediator between God and man so that I'm spared from the justice toward my sins I deserve. Because of the shed blood of Jesus, I instead receive grace and mercy.

Holy Spirit, You are a strong instrument of justice. Thank You for delivering justice on behalf of God and His kingdom agenda on earth. Thank You for Your great wisdom and power of restraint. You know how to use justice so that it produces good and not harm in the lives of those it impacts.

SUPPLICATION

Lord God, I ask for Your justice brought about through the presence of the Holy Spirit to be gentle and an instrument of teaching to those who receive it. Show us all how we can better serve and worship You so that we will draw closer to You and find comfort in You. The Holy Spirit of Justice is for Him who sits in judgment and is a strength to those who repel the onslaught at the gate. Your justice defends me from the unjust attacks of the enemy, and I take comfort in the Spirit of Justice, who reveals Your power to me.

I ask that with the Spirit of Justice You protect me from those who would seek to do me or those I love harm. May the Spirit of Justice let all those around me know that You've chosen me to serve You with my life. You are my defender, and because the Spirit of Justice is my strength and defense and my glory, You will not allow the unjust to gain a stronghold over me. Remove those who come at me to thwart the advancement of Your kingdom rule. Replace them with those who seek Your will and Your glory above all else.

35

The New Spirit

I will give them one heart, and put a new spirit within them. And I will take the heart of stone out of their flesh and give them a heart of flesh.

EZEKIEL 11:19

ADORATION

Father, Your Word speaks of regeneration and renewal. You awaken my soul within me and breathe new life where my light and life have gone out. I look to You to refresh me and revive me. This life and situations in it can produce a callousness of soul, and yet Your Holy Spirit gives new life.

You speak of the New Spirit who comes into our fleshly spirit and heart and gives the eternal spiritual newness of You. This is a result of trusting in Christ alone for the salvation from our sins. You say You'll give those of us in Your body a new heart and a New Spirit within us, taking out and away the heart of stone made from flesh and giving us a heart of Spirit in our flesh, restoring us to Your redemptive plan. I worship You and praise You, for Your name is worthy of all praise, glory, and blessing.

CONFESSION

God, I confess that I operate out of the mindset of my old heart, which is stone, rather than out of the New Spirit You've blessed me with, reviving my life and my mind. Forgive me for bypassing this New Spirit placed in a new heart and thus relying on my flesh and my own thoughts to guide me.

I am made new in You through the gift of the New Spirit, which blesses not only me but all those who call on the name of Jesus to be saved. Forgive me for neglecting such a great gift. Forgive me for failing to recognize all of the great gifts You've given me in the presence and inner working of Your Holy Spirit.

THANKSGIVING

Father, thank You for all You've blessed me with. Thank You for giving me the New Spirit that quickens and awakens the spirit within me, for giving me a new heart to beat in cadence with Your own.

Thank You for teaching me Your ways and honoring me with the intimacy of Your presence. Thank You for knowing all I need and bestowing it upon me through the blessing of the New Spirit. I lift up my new heart full of gratitude and joy, asking that You use me as Your willing servant. I desire to help others find all they have to be grateful for in You as well. Will the New Spirit show me how to do that?

SUPPLICATION

Lord God, I ask to walk in the newness of life, abandoning the ways and mentality of my old heart, which is now a heart of stone. I ask that I be shown Your mighty hand and the ways of my Lord so that I can follow You and find the peace that surpasses all understanding.

Please show me how to honor You with my life. Show me how to demonstrate my new life with the New Spirit in me. Make me an instrument of Your grace and newness to those around me, giving them a greater motivation to seek You and love You above all else. May Your name be glorified and Your kingdom agenda be advanced across all of the earth so that everyone may know You are the one, true God who rules and reigns over all.

36

The Spirit Who Gives Rest

As the cattle which go down into the valley,
the Spirit of the LORD gave them rest.
So You led Your people, to make
for Yourself a glorious name.
ISAIAH 63:14

ADORATION

Father, You lead with such wisdom and insight. You know how we're formed, and You know what we need. As a good shepherd leads his flock to the waters or into the valley, You give us rest. You lead us where we can find restoration for our bodies and our souls. And it's the Holy Spirit who gives us this gift of rest. The Holy Spirit shows me not only my need for rest but how to obtain it.

You've considered all things so that we're able to proclaim Your glorious name throughout the course of our lives. I love You, and I lift Your name in praise, asking that You delight in the worship I offer You right now and always.

CONFESSION

God, I confess that I busy myself and get distracted by doing too many things. I don't even need to do much of what I find myself doing. The pressing needs, however, each vie for my attention, and I try to meet them all. But You know the importance and value of rest. You know that without rest, I'll burn out. You know that for me to maintain my service to You so that Your name may be lifted above all else throughout the world, I need to steward my body with rest.

Forgive me for ignoring the Holy Spirit's leading to rest. Forgive me for pushing the Spirit's wise nudges aside and pushing ahead with my own agenda. Forgive me for neglecting to take care of my body, which is the temple of the Lord. I must care for it so that You can use me to the fullest extent possible.

THANKSGIVING

Father, thank You for rest. Thank You for the opportunity to rest my mind, my body, and my soul. I find rest in You. Your Word gives me peace. Your Holy Spirit leads me like a good shepherd, showing me the importance of rest and how to cherish it.

Thank You for reminders the Holy Spirit sends my way, inviting me to rest. Even in Jesus Christ, I find rest for my soul. Rest is such an important part of the spiritual life, and yet it's often so neglected. Thank You for Your Word that speaks so highly of rest. May I learn and apply Your Word so that I can grow and mature as Your child, led by the Spirit Who Gives Rest.

SUPPLICATION

Lord God, I ask for a greater rest. I ask that I willingly set aside my busy schedule and embrace rest. I pray for this, because I know You sometimes force rest upon those who don't seek it. Help me willingly rest so that I never reach the point of exhaustion or need to be forced to rest.

Holy Spirit, guide me into the pastures of rest God has for me. Restore my soul. Revive my spirit. Strengthen my body through rest. Let rest be a regular way of life for me so that when I do work, I can do so more effectively because I'm working from a place of rest and strength.

37

The Spirit Who Blows like the Wind

*The wind blows where it wishes and you hear the sound
of it, but do not know where it comes from and where
it is going; so is everyone who is born of the Spirit.*

JOHN 3:8

ADORATION

Father, Your ways are mysterious to me. Your ways are mysterious to everyone. You're like the wind that blows where it wishes. I hear the sound of it, but I don't know where it comes from or where it's going. I can't trace it.

Yet You've chosen to invite me into Your mysterious ways through the abiding work of the Holy Spirit. The Spirit Who Blows like the Wind resides in me. I am moved by the Spirit where the Spirit wishes. I don't know from where or where to, and yet the Holy Spirit knows, and I trust Him. I trust that the Spirit who moves me and guides me does so for Your glory and the greater good of humanity. I worship You for this great gift to take part in the work and wonder of God on earth.

CONFESSION

God, I confess this weakness—the desire to know the details of what I'm asked to do or where I'm asked to go. Trust and faith don't come to me as easily as I would like. I want to know the plan rather than trust the One who made it.

But the Holy Spirit guides me like the wind, and it's my desire to follow His leading. So I ask, first, that You forgive me for my trepidation when it comes to not knowing all of the details ahead of time. Let me know the closeness of Your love as Your forgiveness showers me with mercy and grace, thus increasing my faith to follow the leading of the Spirit as He guides and directs me.

THANKSGIVING

Father, thank You for loving me so much that You work in my life to guide me and direct me through the Spirit Who Blows like the Wind. Thank You that I don't have to know all things or figure out all things. Rather, I can trust You. You know all things. You know the best approach to all things. You know how to resolve the issues I face and how to achieve the kingdom purposes You've placed in my heart to pursue.

Holy Spirit, thank You for blowing through me because I am born of the Spirit. Thank You for guiding me like the wind here or there according to the work and will of God.

SUPPLICATION

Lord God, I ask for greater insight into surrender. Surrender allows me to flow with the Holy Spirit, who guides me according to Your will. I ask for a greater trust in the Spirit and communion with Him.

Holy Spirit, make me know Your presence in a way I never have. Let me know You're close by. Let me see and experience the delights that come from following You. Blow as the wind in my life, taking me on a path I've never known, yet a path that will bring God the greatest glory and delight.

38

The Spirit Who Knows God's Thoughts

*Who among men knows the thoughts of a man except
the spirit of the man which is in him? Even so the
thoughts of God no one knows except the Spirit of God.*

1 CORINTHIANS 2:11

ADORATION

Father, Your thoughts are beyond my knowing. And yet the Holy Spirit knows Your thoughts, and He lives in me. The Holy Spirit knows all my thoughts and Yours. He works in my life to help my thoughts align with Yours. He's especially equipped to know how to guide me, because He knows God's thoughts.

Even my spirit deceives me at times, listening to thoughts that aren't my own. Yet the Holy Spirit is never deceived. He discerns all things, and that's how He can teach all truth to the believers who profess in the name of Christ. I worship You, God, for the purity of the Holy Spirit, who knows Your thoughts and is willing to share them with me in ways that help me know You and love You.

CONFESSION

God, I confess that I fail to appreciate the Holy Spirit at the level I should. The Holy Spirit knows Your thoughts, and He's in me by virtue of Jesus Christ and the Savior's death, burial, and resurrection. I confess my sin of leaning on my own understanding rather than seeking the thoughts of God through the illumination of the Holy Spirit and the revelation of Your Word.

Forgive me for skipping over the ways I know help me know Your thoughts, God, instead relying on my own ways and thinking. This has led to much grief and pain in my life. Send Your forgiveness to me for my sins, and cleanse me of all unrighteousness so that I can focus more fully on You and Your will for my life from a place of purity and grace.

THANKSGIVING

Father, thank You for revealing Your thoughts to me through the Holy Spirit. Thank You for making the Holy Spirit an integral part of my life. Thank You for never leaving me nor forsaking me. You're always available to me because of the unique and divinely powerful presence of the Holy Spirit. I worship the Spirit for His guidance and clarity in leading me.

Thank You, Spirit, for Your patience with me and for showing me that I need to grow and mature more spiritually. The thoughts of God are precious and perfect. Thank You for revealing spiritual truth to me as I look to You for instruction.

SUPPLICATION

Lord God, I ask for great wisdom. Wisdom comes from above. Wisdom is rooted in Your thoughts. I ask that the Holy Spirit, who knows Your thoughts, will give me great wisdom. I ask to know in what direction I should go in my life. I ask to know how to hold my tongue and remain quiet. I also ask to know when I should speak up on behalf of truth, justice, and mercy.

Holy Spirit, reveal to me the very thoughts of God that I may know Him more fully. I invite You and Your work into my life at a deeper level than ever before. I long to know the truth of God and make His presence manifest in me.

39

The Spirit Who Testifies We Are God's Children

*The Spirit Himself testifies with our spirit
that we are children of God.*

ROMANS 8:16

ADORATION

Father, You have created the body of Christ like a family. We *are* a family. We're united in love under You. You sit as our God, King, and Lord but also as our Father. I am Your child, and all those who call on Your name and the name of Jesus Christ are Your children. We are siblings together. As a family ought to function, we are to function.

We are to help one another, encourage one another, and defend one another with brotherly love. We're to show up and be there for each other when we can. You thought of all things when You created this Christian family. You sought to provide a way for us to find community so that we can both contribute to it and be blessed by it. I love You, God, and I love the Holy Spirit, who testifies with my spirit that I am Your beloved child, as are all in Christ Jesus.

CONFESSION

God, I confess my neglect of the family, the collective body of Jesus Christ. So many times, I neglect to participate as I should. Yet Your Holy Spirit never neglects to testify to my spirit that I am Your child, and likewise are those who believe in You.

Forgive me for failing to live up to the standards and expectations of a family, for that is what we are under You as our Father. Forgive me for neglecting to share, give, and serve as I ought. Also forgive me for neglecting to reach out when I have a need that can be met by the extended family You've given me through this body of kingdom followers.

THANKSGIVING

Father, thank You for caring for me enough that You've surrounded me with others who are my family in the Lord Jesus Christ. Thank You for the Holy Spirit, who testifies to my spirit so that I know this is true. I know I'm part of something bigger. I'm a special member of an extraordinary family, whose members find our purpose and our mission in You. Thank You that I'm not alone but rather am surrounded by those who love You as I do.

And because of our love for You, we also love one another. This is how the world knows we're Your disciples—because the love in us testifies of this just as the Holy Spirit testifies that we are Your children.

SUPPLICATION

Lord God, I ask for a greater awareness of the Holy Spirit and His testimony in my life. I ask You to help me know Your Spirit in a deeper way. Show me how to communicate with You and the Holy Spirit more intimately and authentically so that I can fully realize the kingdom purpose You've designed me to fulfill.

Holy Spirit, remind me of Your presence. Remind me of Your power. Refresh my love for You in such a way that I think of You and cherish

You more frequently. I want my life to be a pleasing aroma to the God Most High. And Your testimony in me as His child, Holy Spirit, will help me do this.

40

The Spirit Who Heals

To another faith by the same Spirit,
and to another gifts of healing by the one Spirit.
1 CORINTHIANS 12:9

ADORATION

Father, Your creation is perfect, whole and complete. You've given life and given it abundantly. Yet in some seasons ill health plagues us; our physical bodies or our minds struggle. In Your perfection, You've designed this for Your own purposes, purposes we may not understand until eternity. But I trust You and Your ways, and I praise You for knowing how things ought to be.

I also praise You for offering the Spirit Who Can Heal in these seasons of ill health or fragility. Not only can the Holy Spirit heal the body, but He can heal the mind and heart. The Holy Spirit can heal emotions. You've considered all that I need and have provided a way for me to access it through the power of the Spirit Who Heals. I praise and lift up Your name in adoration.

CONFESSION

God, I confess that the Holy Spirit isn't the first place I go when I need physical, mental, or emotional healing. Instead, I run to my medicine cabinet or online to look up what I can do on my own. After that, I may consult a physician. But, Lord, You've given me the Holy Spirit to heal me and my loved ones.

I ask for Your forgiveness in failing to turn to the Holy Spirit in this capacity as much as I should. I should look to Him first and to those You've raised up with the gift of healing insights through the power of the Holy Spirit. Let Your love and mercy revive me, Lord, so that I will walk closely with the Holy Spirit in full health and vitality.

THANKSGIVING

Father, thank You for the Spirit Who Heals. Thank You for those to whom You've given the special gift of the Holy Spirit to have healing insights that can bless the body of Christ at large. Thank You for the wisdom that comes from above, which guides and leads us to navigate ill health or physical or mental fragility on earth.

You've thought of all things, so I want to give You my heart of gratitude. Receive my thanksgiving for all You are and for all the Holy Spirit is and has to offer us in Your collective body of believers. You are a great and mighty God, worthy of the gratitude that comes to You.

SUPPLICATION

Lord God, I ask for the Spirit of Healing to touch my body, mind, and emotions with His healing power to restore me to full health and vitality. Where I harm my body through my own choices or ignorance, I ask for the Spirit of Healing to reveal this to me.

Holy Spirit, show me how to take better care of my body as the temple of the living Lord so that I will live with strength and energy to carry out Your will. Fill me with Your loving care, nurturing my physical, emotional, and mental well-being so that I'm fully vibrant in all ways, a testimony to the King of kings and His power, available to us in so many ways.

41

The Spirit of Fire

There appeared to them tongues as of fire
distributing themselves, and they
rested on each one of them.

ACTS 2:3

ADORATION

Father, Your power comes to me through the presence of the Holy Spirit. You rest Your power and might on me as You did on the disciples at Pentecost. You delivered Your power to them, appearing as tongues of fire, resting on each of them in order to strengthen them and give them a greater confidence in You. Before the Holy Spirit rested on them, they were afraid. They were in a closed room. They hid and wondered what would become of them.

Yet You, Lord, came to them through the mighty fire of the Holy Spirit and empowered them to take Your name and make it known. Once the Holy Spirit rested on them as fire, without fear they proclaimed the name of Jesus Christ and the saving life found in Him. The boldness You give to each of us when the Spirit of Fire is on us enables us to fulfill Your will and advance Your kingdom agenda on this earth.

CONFESSION

God, I confess my lack of boldness when it comes to proclaiming Your name and Your gospel. It's a calling You've given to each of us who follow You and call upon the name of Jesus for the salvation of our souls.

And yet some days, weeks, and even months I don't share Your gospel with anyone. Forgive me for failing to pray for the Spirit of Fire to embolden me. Forgive me for looking to my own flesh to give me the strength to be Your ambassador. I can't do this great task in my own strength. I need the Spirit of Fire just as the early disciples did. I'm no different, and yet at times I forget that. Have mercy on me so that I can receive Your forgiveness and find the strength to pray for the boldness I need to proclaim Your name to those I can.

THANKSGIVING

Father, thank You for the Spirit of Fire, who gives me the ability to do so much more than I could ever do on my own. Thank You for Your provision of courage, strength, and spiritual gifts made available to me through the Holy Spirit. You've thought of everything I've needed, and You've set me up for spiritual success if I will but follow Your leading and seek the Spirit of Fire to strengthen me.

Thank You for the great privilege of telling of the saving grace of Jesus Christ as I go about my days. I want to make known Your name and the Scriptures through which You set us free, instructing and encouraging others on how to know You and follow You as true kingdom disciples.

SUPPLICATION

Lord God, I ask for Your favor. I ask that You bless me with the Spirit of Fire as favor from above, anointing and strengthening me to be an instrument of testimony regarding Jesus Christ, my Savior. I ask that You open doors for me to proclaim the name of Jesus far and wide.

Give me wisdom as the Spirit of Fire rests on me. Give me courage through the Spirit of Fire. Show me abilities I don't even know I have that I may make my life count for Your kingdom as I further the name of Jesus Christ and His saving grace so that all people may know.

42

The Spirit Flowing Within

He who believes in Me, as the Scripture said,
"From his innermost being will flow rivers of living water."
JOHN 7:38

ADORATION

Father, Your presence is all I desire. I want to be near You and hear Your guidance as I go about my days. Sometimes I feel empty, dry, and barren, and this is when Your presence is needed more than ever. I worship You because You've considered all things. You've thought about my needs even before I know what they are. You've provided for me streams of living water that come into me and flow through me as Your Holy Spirit.

I worship You and adore You, my God, for Your gifts are all I need. Your life-giving Spirit floods me with living water so that I can be refreshed. When opposition comes against me or I face spiritual attacks, I look to the Holy Spirit, who flows in me as living water to keep me satisfied and refreshed, aware of Your presence and of the victory that's mine in Christ Jesus.

CONFESSION

God, I confess that my weariness and despair are often a result of failing to fully tap into the Holy Spirit's provision of living water within me. When I feel spiritually parched, it's not because You lack anything or You've neglected to supply me with what I need. I always have enough to nourish me spiritually. It's only a matter of tuning in to the Holy Spirit and drinking from the spiritual living water He gives me.

Forgive me for far too often neglecting this great provision and seeking to go it alone. Have mercy on me as I rush ahead in life, often neglecting the rest and restoration You supply for me on a regular basis.

THANKSGIVING

Father, thank You for the living water that flows in my innermost being. Thank You that the Holy Spirit flows in me like a river, bringing nourishment to my soul and life to my spirit. The Holy Spirit is a gift who supplies the living water I need to face what is in front of me, showering me with peace, joy, kindness, love, courage, and so much more.

Thank You, Holy Spirit, for supplying me with what I need and never running dry. You are a life-giving river, and because of You, I can bloom and grow spiritually so that I can carry out the work of the Lord and fulfill my kingdom purpose on earth.

SUPPLICATION

Lord God, I ask for Your love to be made manifest in me through an awakening of my spirit to know and understand all that You have for me, including the Holy Spirit's living water in me. Awaken my spirit to realize all You've supplied. I want to access Your gift of the Holy Spirit more frequently so that I can benefit from this flowing river within me.

Cause the living water to touch every area of my innermost being, healing my pain and developing my spiritual gifts. I know as I grow and develop, I will serve You and bring You the glory due Your great name.

43

The Spirit from God

Now we have received,
not the spirit of the world, but the Spirit who is from God,
so that we may know the things freely given to us by God.
1 CORINTHIANS 2:12

ADORATION

Father, You've freely given me so many things that give life to my soul and strength to my spirit. The hidden riches of Your blessings are available to me if I will but recognize them and ask for them. The Spirit of God reveals these riches to me, and I praise You for giving Him to me so that He can make me aware of Your provision in my life.

I desire greater wisdom, courage, and faith. But the Holy Spirit knows I have need of even more. I praise You for giving me the opportunity to expand my desires into what I don't even know to seek. The Spirit of God will guide me and show me all I need to know to find my kingdom purpose and live out my destiny so that others can benefit and You can receive Your great glory.

CONFESSION

God, I confess that I know little of Your great and many blessings. I confess that my awareness is sheltered, and I don't even know what to ask for. Unleash Your spiritual blessings into my soul, and let the holy Spirit of God be a constant reminder to me to ask You for more.

Forgive me for failing to ask You for greater patience, greater diligence, and greater wisdom. I should ask these of You every morning, and yet I so often start my day without so much as seeking the higher virtues of Your kingdom and all that You supply. Shower Your mercy and forgiveness onto my soul so that I am washed clean and renewed. I want to know You and all that You've chosen and designated to freely give me.

THANKSGIVING

Father, thank You for Your love. Thank You for choosing to freely give me all things. Thank You for placing within me not the spirit of the world but the Spirit who is from You. Within me lies the Holy Spirit who can make me aware of all I need to know. Thank You for how You've grown me spiritually over the years. I've seen Your hand bring me from afar and draw me close to You. Thank You for Your ongoing and continual work in my life so that I can realize the Holy Spirit's many blessings within.

Holy Spirit, continue to reveal to me all that God, the Father, has freely given me. Help me know even what to pray for and seek. Thank You, Holy Spirit, for your closeness and intimacy as You speak to my soul.

SUPPLICATION

Lord God, I ask for Your favor. Will You send it to me in that which You've chosen to freely give me?

Let me see and witness Your favor in my life. Cause me to marvel at all You've chosen to freely give me. I want to experience it all; do not hold back. Show me how my life can be a blessing to others, teaching them how to experience You, Your love, and Your free blessings.

44

The Spirit of Life

The law of the Spirit of life in Christ Jesus
has set you free from the law of sin and of death.

ROMANS 8:2

ADORATION

Father, You've set me free from the law of sin and death through providing the law of the Spirit of life in Christ Jesus, my Lord. I worship and adore You for how You've given me this freedom and made me know Your grace. This grace causes me to lift Your name on high.

You are the mighty God who covers and provides for all. You do not wish that I stay stuck in guilt, sin, or death. It's not Your desire for any of us to fail or live in bondage. That's why You sent Your Holy Spirit from above—to make the way toward freedom. The Holy Spirit liberates me from the law of sin and death, placing me in a position of joy, hope, and delight.

CONFESSION

God, I confess that I focus on the law of sin and death, which causes me great guilt and grief. When I sin against You, I often hold the guilt from that sin longer than I should, and it causes me to live in bondage, regret, and fear. Shame covers me rather than Your grace because I choose to focus on that from which You've set me free.

Your Spirit of life in Christ Jesus is what gives me forgiveness and newness of life. Forgive me for looking at the law rather than at the life of Christ. Forgive me for wasting my days and my thoughts on guilt and shame when You've freely forgiven me and set me loose to pursue a life of godliness in You.

THANKSGIVING

Father, thank You for the freedom that's mine in Christ Jesus through the Holy Spirit and His work in my life. Thank You that I don't need to remain a slave to the law. My members are not bound to the law. I'm free from shame and guilt because of the holy Spirit of life in Christ Jesus. Thank You for the courage to walk with my head held high, knowing I'm a beloved child of the King. You lift my spirit and my life in such a way that causes my heart to overflow with gratitude.

Receive my thanksgiving, Holy Spirit, for how You've set me free from the law of sin and death, renewing my spirit so that I can commit myself as a living sacrifice, holy and pleasing to the Lord.

SUPPLICATION

Lord God, I ask for the freedom You've given me through the powerful presence of the Holy Spirit to be ever before my heart and mind. Send me reminders of Your love and freedom through the Holy Spirit. Help me recognize the Spirit who gives me life, to honor Him and spend my days in quiet companionship with Him.

I want to live a peaceful life as You've called me to in Your Word. But too often, shame and guilt create pain. Release me from shame and guilt, because You've set me free through the Holy Spirit and His work in me. Let me experience this freedom in my everyday life.

45

The Holy Spirit Power of the Most High

The angel answered and said to her,
"The Holy Spirit will come upon you,
and the power of the Most High will overshadow you;
and for that reason the holy Child
shall be called the Son of God."

LUKE 1:35

ADORATION

Father, Your power can produce all things. Your power spoke the world into existence. Your power creates life. You create all things. When You send Your Holy Spirit to come upon or remain in anyone, Your power is accessed.

What a gift You've given to each of us who have found salvation through faith alone in Christ alone. What a blessing You've bestowed upon me for my salvation and the dwelling of the Spirit within me. You give me life and also the ability to enjoy it through Your loving care and presence of the Holy Spirit. I bless Your name, for the Holy Spirit Power of the Most High is a gift indescribable.

CONFESSION

God, I confess that I haven't honored You or thanked You enough for the many blessings You've given me, including how the Holy Spirit Power of the Most High lives within me, causing my spirit to come alive.

Forgive me for neglecting to thank You and recognize what a great gift and honor it is to have the Holy Spirit in my life, able to help me in any way possible so that I can fulfill Your plan for me. Thank You for Your Holy Word, which teaches me about the Holy Spirit. When the Holy Spirit Power of the Most High came upon Mary, she received the miracle conception of Jesus Christ. You are great and worthy to be praised.

THANKSGIVING

Father, thank You for Your perfect plan of salvation. Thank You for sending the Holy Spirit Power of the Most High to overshadow Mary so that Jesus Christ could come to earth, born of a virgin. Thank You for giving us the gift of salvation through Christ's atonement for our sins. This same Holy Spirit who visited Mary is available to me to work miracles in my life so that I can serve You more fully. Thank You for opening my eyes to see that the Holy Spirit has power from You, which makes me able to carry out the plan You've destined and ordained for me.

Holy Spirit, fill me with great wisdom and power from the Most High so that I can be a pleasing sacrifice to You.

SUPPLICATION

Lord God, I ask for Your power, the power of the Most High, to anoint my mind, thoughts, and actions. Show me how I can serve You more fully and bring You more glory. Let me see Your pleasure and feel Your delight. I ask that the power of the Most High will cause me to rise up with great courage to live a life that honors You in all things.

Teach me how to worship You in ways that bring You joy. Teach me how to delight You with my spiritual service of worship. Mary served You through bearing Christ on earth. I, too, want to serve You in great ways that will spread the gospel around the world.

46

The Spirit Who Seals

Who also sealed us and gave us the
Spirit in our hearts as a pledge.
2 CORINTHIANS 1:22

ADORATION

Father, Your Spirit seals us. You've given us the Holy Spirit in our hearts as a pledge, and the Spirit's seal can't be broken. Man can't take it away. I don't need to fear losing my relationship with You, because You've provided it for me through the shed blood of Jesus Christ.

I worship and adore You for Your provision of the seal of the Holy Spirit, who brings me comfort and peace. I don't need to worry. Your love has provided me with the protection and assurance I need to live in a way that's free from fear of loss of my relationship with You. I give You praise, for You are a patient, kind, and giving God who has thought of everything ahead of time, sealing Your purpose and presence through the Holy Spirit.

CONFESSION

God, I confess that I don't always think about the Holy Spirit as a seal of Your loving presence in me. But He's a pledge given to my heart to assure me of my salvation and my relationship with You through the blood of Jesus and His sacrifice on the cross.

Forgive me for when doubts creep in and begin to consume my thinking. Forgive me for trying so hard to live the perfect Christian life on my own when You've sealed me in Your Spirit. You've offered me all I need for spiritual growth and wisdom through the presence of the Spirit, who seals me in You. Please show me forgiveness for my lack of awareness and understanding of how the Spirit can work in my life, and help me understand more fully.

THANKSGIVING

Father, thank You for Your loving care that assures me of my salvation through the seal of the Spirit. Thank You for making salvation possible through the sacrifice of the sinless Savior, Jesus Christ. I offer up a heart of gratitude for all You've done, continue to do, and promise to do in the future through this Spirit Who Seals.

You are a mighty God, and I thank You for allowing me to know You personally.

SUPPLICATION

Lord God, I ask for greater assurance of my relationship with You. You've given me this assurance through the Spirit Who Seals, but I ask to know this on a greater level personally.

Reveal Your faithful love to me in ways I can't argue or dismiss. I want to see and experience You on a whole new level because of the closeness of the Spirit Who Seals. Guide me in ways that give me the opportunity to know You more. Help me be a testament to others of Your great name and glorious movement in Your children's lives. Cause me to be an instrument of grace to those around me so that their fears are diminished and their assurance in You is increased.

The Spirit Who Washes, Sanctifies, and Justifies

You were washed, but you were sanctified,
but you were justified in the name of the Lord Jesus Christ
and in the Spirit of our God.
1 CORINTHIANS 6:11

ADORATION

Father, Your holiness is like none other. You are holy, spotless, and pure. You live a blameless existence, and all that is good comes from You. When I want to see what purity looks and lives like, I only have to look to You.

Yet I am a sinner. My flesh often draws me away from the holiness You've called me to. But You've sought to address this through the work of the Holy Spirit. The Holy Spirit has been sent to wash Your children and sanctify us. We're justified in the name of the Lord Jesus Christ and in the Holy Spirit of God. I lift up Your name in adoration, for You have thoughts of all things, even a way to purify sinners so we can be close in Your presence every moment of each day.

CONFESSION

God, I confess that I have many sins that need to be forgiven and washed away. I have much in my heart that's rooted in sinfulness. Forgive me for my pride, jealousy, and malice.

Forgive me for my apathy when it comes to Your will and Your work. Forgive me for all of my sins that I may be washed clean and made new. It's because of the shed blood of Jesus Christ that I'm forgiven. I'm sanctified and justified in Christ and in Your Holy Spirit. Your forgiveness gives me the ability to hold up my head and live boldly for Your name and to advance Your glory.

THANKSGIVING

Father, thank You for Your loving care in providing me with a way to be forgiven for my sins and made clean. You've thought of all things, especially my need to be washed by the blood of Jesus and cleansed by the Holy Spirit. Sanctify me in Your truth and in Your Word. Let the Spirit guide my thoughts and my mind so that I understand and am able to live a life that's pleasing to You.

Thank You, God, for giving me the priceless gift of the Spirit. Thank You for the forgiveness and cleansing power You've blessed me with. Thank You that I'm a child of the King and that You have a good plan for my life, as I trust in You and Your sanctifying power.

SUPPLICATION

Lord God, I ask for Your cleansing power to rid me of the pain and consequences of my sin. Have mercy on me so that I may see Your face and delight as I serve You. I want to live a pure and blameless life, and yet my flesh often rears its ugly head and draws me astray.

Let Your Holy Spirit sanctify me and bless me with the washing and renewal of my spirit within. Let the sacrifice of Jesus Christ be made evident in my life to such a degree that I spend my days in gratitude and service to You. I never want to forget the gifts You've given me and the way You guide me throughout my life, giving me opportunities to know and serve You as a beloved child of the King.

48

The Spirit of Power, Love, and Discipline

God has not given us a spirit of timidity,
but of power and love and discipline.

2 TIMOTHY 1:7

ADORATION

Father, You haven't given me a spirit of timidity. When I feel fear and anxiety, they're not from You. And when I lack the courage to stand up for my faith and beliefs, that lack is not from You. You've given me the Holy Spirit, who bestows power, love, and discipline. This discipline reflects a sound mind and guides me in all I do. I worship You, for Your ways are far above my own. Your courage is never-ending. You are a strong, holy, and mighty God.

I worship You, Holy Spirit, for You are the embodiment of all that is good, noble, pure, and true.

CONFESSION

God, I confess that I lack the courage I need to always stand up for my beliefs. Sometimes I find it easy, but other times I remain quiet when I should speak up. Or I go with the flow rather than make decisions that would honor You more.

Forgive me for going along with the world's ways when I shouldn't. Your Holy Spirit is good to convict me in those times, but I often ignore the conviction out of fear. Please send Your forgiveness to me and give me the courage to live as a committed follower of Jesus Christ.

THANKSGIVING

Father, thank You for giving me power to overcome timidity. Thank You for showing me that the Holy Spirit offers me a spirit of power, love, and a sound mind. I can live a life of personal discipline because I have the Holy Spirit in me. I don't need to give in to the ways of the world or the influences of culture. I have the Holy Spirit, who gives me courage to do what is right and best in the moment, in me.

The Holy Spirit empowers me in so many ways. I'm thankful for His ongoing presence and equipping in my life.

SUPPLICATION

Lord God, I ask for greater power when it comes to following You. I ask that I understand what it means to lean on the Holy Spirit on a deeper level so that timidity, anxiety, and fear no longer consume me. Show me how to communicate with the Holy Spirit on a regular basis so that I walk according to the way of the Holy Spirit. Open my heart and enlighten my eyes to know You and the power of the Spirit that lives in me.

Make me an instrument that extends Your love and care to a world in need. I want to advance Your kingdom agenda on earth. Reveal to me how I can do this. Grant me the courage to take the steps I need to in order to live out my purpose and calling for Your glory and the greater good of all mankind.

49

The Promise

*In order that in Christ Jesus the blessing of Abraham
might come to the Gentiles, so that we would
receive the promise of the Spirit through faith.*

GALATIANS 3:14

ADORATION

Father, Your Word gives us so many wonderful promises. One of the best is Your promise of eternal life for those who put their faith alone in Christ alone for the forgiveness of their sins. Through Jesus, the blessing of Abraham may come even to the Gentiles so that they will receive the promise of the Spirit through faith.

Not only is eternal life promised for those who believe in Jesus Christ and His sacrifice on the cross, but the promise of the blessed Holy Spirit is made available as well. You haven't limited Your presence of the Holy Spirit to a certain people group but made Him available to anyone who calls on the name of the Lord Jesus Christ so that they may be saved.

CONFESSION

God, I confess my sin of disbelief and lack of faith when it comes to how much access I have to You through the promise of the Holy Spirit. I confess that my doubt has stopped me from boldly approaching Your throne of grace in prayer.

Forgive me for holding back when because I've placed my faith alone in Christ alone for the salvation of my soul, You've made the promised gift of Your Holy Spirit available to me at any time. Please reveal to me Your generous forgiveness so that I'll experience what it feels like to walk closely with the Holy Spirit each day.

THANKSGIVING

Father, thank You for the promise of the Holy Spirit, who comes to me through Jesus Christ and His gift of salvation. Thank You for honoring me with Your presence and the promise of the Holy Spirit. Thank You for making Yourself available to me so that I can have the power and courage to serve You.

Calm my doubts and remove my shame so that I will boldly approach Your throne of grace to ask what I need to ask in prayer. I don't want to hold back. Your promise of the Holy Spirit assures me of the blessings of Abraham, which I can access as well because I'm Your child due to Jesus' sacrifice.

SUPPLICATION

Lord God, I ask for greater grace to know the Holy Spirit and the blessings of Abraham, which are mine. I ask for greater wisdom as I pray.

Show me how to pray in a way that taps into Your promises for my life. Unleash the promise of the Holy Spirit in me so that I can fully feel His presence. I want to know You more, so I ask that the Holy Spirit make You known to me and guide me into receiving the blessings of Abraham.

50

The Spirit of Prophecy

*I fell at his feet to worship him. But he said to me, "Do
not do that; I am a fellow servant of yours and your
brethren who hold the testimony of Jesus; worship God.
For the testimony of Jesus is the spirit of prophecy."*

REVELATION 19:10

ADORATION

Father, the testimony of Jesus is the Spirit of Prophecy. You know the beginning and the end. When I have questions, it's Your Spirit who guides me. We're not to worship or glorify anyone other than You, because You're the one who knows what is to come. You are the keeper of all truth. The testimony of Jesus and the Spirit of Prophecy are made available to each of us through an intimate and abiding relationship with You.

I praise You because You are all-knowing and ever-present, and You allow me to have a relationship with You according to Your divine power and perfect will. Guide me in the path that brings You pleasure, and help me understand the work of the Spirit of Prophecy in my life on a greater level.

CONFESSION

God, I confess that I often wonder about what is to come, and then that wonder turns into worry. Sometimes I spend a significant amount of my time anxious because of my questions and concerns about what the future holds. I wonder about Your plans, the spiritual battles to take place, and when Jesus will return to usher us all into Your presence in eternity.

Forgive me for worrying when I have You and Your Holy Spirit of Prophecy, who abides in me as a dear friend. You are my God, yet You also make Yourself known to me, and I ask for Your forgiveness for forgetting this and turning to worry instead.

THANKSGIVING

Father, thank You for guiding me and showing me things to come through Your Holy Word. Thank You for the revelation of Your Word and the Spirit of Prophecy. I want to understand Your Word more fully, so I begin by offering You a heart of gratitude for Your illumination and revelation. Help me know Your work and Your works to come.

Thank You for the loving presence of the Holy Spirit and how He is the Spirit of Prophecy, available to me in a relationship because of the shed blood of Jesus Christ.

SUPPLICATION

Lord God, I ask to know Your will and Your way and Your plans. I ask to know the Spirit of Prophecy on such a level that it helps me understand Your Scripture and where You speak of what is to come. Enlighten my heart and eyes to gain insight into Your plans for the future. I don't want to live in fear of the future or even in fear of the present day.

Give me a spirit of calm as I look to Your Spirit of Prophecy to guide me and direct me into each new day, knowing that the Spirit knows where I'm to go and what is to unfold according to Your will and eternal plan.

51

The Spirit Who Abides in You

That is the Spirit of truth, whom the world cannot receive,
because it does not see Him or know Him,
but you know Him because He abides
with you and will be in you.

JOHN 14:17

ADORATION

Father, Your Holy Spirit is the Spirit of truth whom those of the world can't receive because they don't see Him or know Him. I know the Holy Spirit because He abides in me and is with me as I go throughout my days.

I worship You, Father, for Your provision of the Holy Spirit, who abides with me. As I am to abide in Jesus Christ, I also receive the abiding presence of the Holy Spirit, who helps me abide in Christ. The Holy Spirit draws me close to You so that I can more fully understand who You are and discover ways to serve You and please You in all I do.

CONFESSION

God, I confess my weariness as I go through the days when I'm not abiding in Christ and not acknowledging the Holy Spirit, who abides in me. I confess that these times are empty, and they often lead to confusion. And yet You've given me access to life, hope, and abundance through this gift of abiding with You through the presence of the Holy Spirit and Jesus Christ.

Forgive me for neglecting to nurture my relationship with Jesus Christ and with You through the abiding presence of the Holy Spirit. Forgive me for being so easily distracted that I forget this great gift You've given me to experience and enjoy.

THANKSGIVING

Father, thank You for Your endearing and enduring love given to me through the offer of abiding in Jesus Christ. You've placed in me the Holy Spirit, who abides in me, and through Him, I come to know You even more. I hope in You even more. I understand You even more. I worship You even more. The Spirit of truth, who abides in me, helps me discern what's right and what's wrong and helps bring me peace so that I don't need to fear what the world seeks to frighten me with.

Thank You for Your assurance and comfort, which come to my heart and soul through the abiding presence of the Holy Spirit, who loves me and reflects Your presence in me.

SUPPLICATION

Lord God, I ask for Your favor made manifest to me through the abiding presence of the Holy Spirit of truth. Make Your truth known to me on a level deeper than I've ever experienced.

Show me how to study Your Word more thoroughly. Guide me into levels of discernment so that I can distinguish between the deception of the enemy and the truth of my God and Savior. Let the abiding power of the Holy Spirit open my eyes to see You more clearly and hear from You more fully. I want to live a life that pleases You and accomplishes the goals and destiny You have for my life. Show me what You would have me do with the time You've given me. I love You and praise You, my King and my God.

52

The Holy Spirit of God

Do not grieve the Holy Spirit of God,
by whom you were sealed for the day of redemption.
EPHESIANS 4:30

ADORATION

Father, Your love is precious, and Your provision is complete. You've given me all I need to live the abundant Christian life through the gift of the Holy Spirit of God. The Holy Spirit allows me to know You and draw close to You, and yet I can do things that grieve the Holy Spirit. When I sin, I grieve the Holy Spirit and bring Him pain.

I praise You for revealing this truth to me so that I won't go about my days without this awareness. I don't want to grieve the Holy Spirit of God or bring Him pain. I worship You for opening my eyes to this reality through the truth found in Your Word.

CONFESSION

God, I confess that I've grieved the Holy Spirit through my sinful actions and thoughts. Forgive me for sinning against You and bringing pain to the Holy Spirit, who is Your gift to help me live out my life in peace, grace, and growth.

Forgive me for failing You in so many ways. Forgive me for taking Your forgiveness lightly at times so that I grieve the Holy Spirit again by repeating sins for which You've shown me forgiveness. I ask for Your forgiveness to cleanse both my heart and my mind so that repentance will be real in me and I'll truly turn away from the sins I've committed and am tempted to commit.

THANKSGIVING

Father, thank You for the Holy Spirit of God, who has sealed me for the day of redemption and allows me to understand the gravity of sin on a level I wouldn't know without the Him and His work in my life. Thank You that even though I've grieved the Holy Spirit with my sin, He has not left me and will not abandon me. Thank You for the promise of Your presence and the gift of Your grace.

My heart swells with gratitude as I think about the many gifts You've blessed me with through the presence of the Holy Spirit, who lives in me and abides in me.

SUPPLICATION

Lord God, I ask for wisdom and restraint so that I won't sin as I've done. I want to live a holy and pure life blameless before You so that I won't grieve the Holy Spirit, who's given me so many blessings. I want a close relationship with the Holy Spirit, enjoying each other's company every moment.

Show me how to nurture my relationship with the Holy Spirit in a way that causes me to be aware of His presence and leads me away from temptation and sin. I want to please You with my thoughts and choices, so I ask You to help me walk in the Spirit so that I won't carry out the desires of my flesh, thus grieving the Holy Spirit of God. He is a gift to me.

53

The Spirit Who Instructs

*Which things we also speak,
not in words taught by human wisdom,
but in those taught by the Spirit,
combining spiritual thoughts with spiritual words.*

1 CORINTHIANS 2:13

ADORATION

Father, Your instruction is critical for me to know how to go about my life in a way that pleases You, glorifies You, and brings good to others. Thank You for the instruction You provide me through the presence of the Holy Spirit.

I worship and adore You, because You've made me to know things I could not have known apart from You. You've established the heavens, and You declare the truth we're to live by. It is by Your word that the world is formed and holds together. I praise You because of Your great knowledge and power. The Holy Spirit teaches me not in human wisdom but in spiritual wisdom so that my spirit grows and matures into a fully developed kingdom disciple.

CONFESSION

God, I lack spiritual wisdom on my own. Spiritual wisdom comes from You. Yet I confess that sometimes I forget to ask for it or I think I know a better answer than Yours.

Forgive me for my pride that causes me to neglect seeking the Holy Spirit, who instructs me with spiritual wisdom and gives me insights into Your greatness and power. Have mercy on me for leaning on my own way and depending on worldly wisdom. The Holy Spirit is available to me whenever I need spiritual guidance and instruction, and yet I look to other people to guide me in many moments of my days. Forgive me for neglecting so great a gift as the Holy Spirit in me.

THANKSGIVING

Father, thank You for the Holy Spirit and His wisdom, which helps me know how to live my life and make the most of the time You've given me on this earth. Thank You for giving me a unique calling that will advance Your kingdom agenda and bring about good and benefit for others.

Show me how to honor You more through an ongoing heart of gratitude. Cause me to thank You more regularly by opening my eyes to see how You guide me through the Spirit's leading and instruction.

SUPPLICATION

Lord God, I ask for Your instruction made known to me through the presence of the Holy Spirit. Help me recognize the Holy Spirit and His voice so that I can gain wisdom and guidance and live my life spiritually strategic. Cause me to listen to the Spirit on a more regular basis so that His communication to me becomes second nature and is a natural way for me to gain insight and learning.

Grow my levels of spiritual discernment so that I can honor You with my life and choices. Help me help others know how to listen to the Holy Spirit more so they can also benefit from a closer relationship with You.

54

The Spirit of Jesus Christ

*I know that this will turn out for my deliverance
through your prayers and the provision
of the Spirit of Jesus Christ.*
PHILIPPIANS 1:19

ADORATION

Father, Your Holy Spirit is the Spirit of Jesus Christ, and I know that whatever I walk through and go through will turn out for my deliverance through the provision of the Spirit. Jesus Christ came to earth to live as a loving sacrifice, giving Himself up for all who will trust in Him for the forgiveness of their sins. He died on the cross so that we may have life and gain access to Him through the Spirit of Jesus Christ, the Holy Spirit, who now makes His home in each of us who believe.

I worship You, Father, for Your provision and plan—and for knowing all we would need to go through life on earth pursuing Your perfect will so that You may be glorified.

CONFESSION

God, I confess that I haven't always lived in a way that's pleasing to You. I've followed my own path and given in to temptations more than I would like to admit, but You know the truth and how I've strayed from You.

Yet the Holy Spirit, whom You've given me, is the Holy Spirit of Jesus Christ, who reminds me of Your perfect salvation and gracious forgiveness. When I ask, You freely forgive. I worship and thank You for Your forgiveness and cleansing power.

THANKSGIVING

Father, thank You for the Holy Spirit of Jesus Christ, who allows the very character of Christ to be made manifest in my life as I seek to abide in Him. I'm able to live a life that reflects Jesus Christ through love, service, humility, and dedication to the expansion of Your will and Your glory.

Thank You for giving me this relationship with Jesus through the Holy Spirit of Jesus Christ so that I'm never alone. I'm always loved. I'm always supplied with all I need, according to Your Word.

SUPPLICATION

Lord God, I ask that Jesus Christ and His perfect life be made known to me through the presence of the Spirit of Jesus Christ in me. I want to know Jesus more intimately and hear what makes Him glad.

Help me reflect Jesus in all I do and say. Convict me of what would not please Him so that I can turn away from it and repent. Show me how to make Jesus known in all I do and say. I want my heart to reflect the heart of Christ with humility, grace, and service toward others. Teach me how to study the Scriptures, so that in them I can see Jesus Christ and His teachings on a greater level. Enable me to live as a kingdom follower of Jesus Christ, advancing the kingdom agenda on earth. Open opportunities for me to serve You where I work and make Jesus Christ known to those I encounter throughout the course of my days.

55

The First Fruits of the Spirit

We ourselves, having the first fruits of the Spirit,
even we ourselves groan within ourselves,
waiting eagerly for our adoption as sons,
the redemption of our body.

ROMANS 8:23

ADORATION

Father, Your presence means more to me than life itself. I praise You for making a way for me to be near You even as I wait for the redemption of my body unto eternal life. I have the first fruits of the Spirit, the promise of what is to come. When I abide with the Holy Spirit, I get a taste of what is to come. I sense Your nearness, and it brings me calm, clarity, and rest.

In You is found the love I long for. In You is the companionship I desire. You are my God, but You are also my friend. I bless Your holy name for giving me a glimpse into You more fully through the first fruits of the Holy Spirit, who is near to me in every way.

CONFESSION

God, I confess that I go through life often dismissing the first fruits of the Holy Spirit and failing to recognize the gift that's mine through the

Spirit's presence in me. I sometimes go through an entire day without recognizing or communing with the Holy Spirit. These days are wasted, because without the first fruits of the Spirit, I'm navigating blindly. I'm walking and speaking in my own strength and worldly wisdom.

Forgive me for when I don't access what You've supplied me through the first fruits of the Holy Spirit.

THANKSGIVING

Father, thank You for loving me enough to send Jesus Christ to live a sinless life on earth and then go to the cross as a sacrifice for the forgiveness of my sins. Thank You that because of Christ's love and holy sacrifice, I gain entrance into the afterlife that allows me to spend it with You forever.

The Holy Spirit is a reminder to me of the beauty of what is to come. Thank You for the gift of the Holy Spirit, who's given me a taste of the redemption of my body and the closeness I will one day experience with You. My heart is full of gratitude for Your presence, love, and purity, made manifest to me through my connection with the Holy Spirit, who dwells within.

SUPPLICATION

Lord God, I ask that Your goodness and grace be made known to me even greater than before. As I wait for the redemption of my body and the access to eternity with You through the sacrifice of Jesus Christ, I look to the Holy Spirit, who is the first fruits of what is to come. I ask for a greater peace, knowing and resting in the truths of Your Holy Word.

Help me know Your Word and find great comfort in it. Show me how I can benefit more fully from the Holy Spirit in me. Teach me the names of the Holy Spirit and all of His character attributes so I can come to know Him at a deeper level.

56

The Spirit of Strength

The Spirit of the LORD will rest on Him,
the spirit of wisdom and understanding,
the spirit of counsel and strength,
the spirit of knowledge and the fear of the LORD.

ISAIAH 11:2

ADORATION

Father, Your strength knows no bounds. Your power has no limits. You are the great, mighty King who reigns and rules over all. I lift Your name in honor and glory and find peace and comfort knowing that You are the great God who covers all. I don't need to fear what the enemy can do to me, because I'm looked after by the Spirit of Strength.

This same Spirit came to Christ when He walked on the earth. This Spirit of Strength, the Holy Spirit, rested on Him as the Spirit of not only strength but of wisdom, understanding, counsel, knowledge, and the fear of the Lord. Jesus has given me the ability to abide in the Holy Spirit of Strength, who now lives in me because of my relationship with my Savior, who gave His life that I might receive the forgiveness of my sins.

CONFESSION

God, I confess that, at times, I neglect to lean on the Holy Spirit of Strength when I need Your strength. Instead, I look to myself to carry me through. But my strength offers no comparison to Yours. That's why I often find myself falling short of Your standards for me. I find myself lacking.

Forgive me for failing to depend on You as I should. You've made all provisions for me, and yet I move through my life lacking so much as a result of my ineptitude in fully living a life solely dependent on You. You are a merciful God with great love. Let Your mercy remind me to depend more on the Spirit of Strength, who's given me every opportunity to tap into Your strength at all times—especially when I need it most.

THANKSGIVING

Father, thank You for the Holy Spirit, a gift sent from above who infuses me with Your strength, wisdom, understanding, and so much more. Thank You for looking out for all of my needs so that I understand how to navigate life.

Reveal to me ways I can depend on You more, especially in those times when I neglect the Holy Spirit's presence in me. Thank You for revealing ways I can be reminded so that I make the most of the Holy Spirit's gifts and provisions within me.

SUPPLICATION

Lord God, I ask for Your Spirit of Strength to give me the strength I need to go through the life challenges I face.

I ask for Your strength to cope and remain courageous in times of fear. Give me strength to overcome any anxious thoughts. I pray for strength to live a life that is holy and devoted to You. I ask for strength to dedicate my thoughts and actions to You. Show me how to honor You with my life, and give me the Spirit of Strength and understanding, which will enable me to make choices that bring You the greatest glory throughout my days.

57

The Spirit Who Seeks the Will of God

*He who searches the hearts knows what the mind
of the Spirit is, because He intercedes for the saints
according to the will of God.*

ROMANS 8:27

ADORATION

Father, Your will is not to be kept secret. You've given the Holy Spirit, who knows Your will. He intercedes on my behalf according to Your will. He knows all things and allows me to know Your will by revealing it to me.

I worship You for not keeping Your will hidden from me. I honor You for providing the Holy Spirit, who serves to intercede on my behalf so that my life can be guided and directed in such a way that will bring You honor and delight. You are the great God who's provided for me in such a way that I can pursue my kingdom calling and not lack anything to live it out.

CONFESSION

God, I confess that I pursue my path and seek my own will far more often than I seek Yours. It's easy for me to rely on my own thoughts, desires, and vision. I look to myself to show me what to do, but then I often regret doing so because only Your will is perfect.

Forgive me for relying on myself rather than on Your Holy Spirit to show me which way to go. Forgive me for underutilizing the Holy Spirit in my life. Forgive my pride, which causes me to think I know which way is best and that I can figure out what Your will is on my own. I can't. I need the Holy Spirit's guidance in my life, and I need the Holy Spirit to intercede on my behalf.

THANKSGIVING

Father, thank You for Your care and Your love. Thank You for Your revelation of truth made known to me through the Holy Spirit. The Holy Spirit searches the heart and knows how to guide me. The Holy Spirit intercedes for me according to Your divine will. The Holy Spirit knows my purpose and kingdom calling.

Thank You for not keeping me in the dark, instead providing an avenue to understanding Your will for my life through my relationship with the Holy Spirit.

SUPPLICATION

Lord God, I ask for the Holy Spirit to intercede on my behalf in ways I don't even know how to ask.

Intercede for me, Holy Spirit, so that my life will be a pleasing aroma to the Lord. Intercede for me so that I will understand how to carry out my days. Intercede for me so that I will grow, develop, and mature spiritually. Intercede for me so that I will understand what the will of God is and how to live according to it. Intercede for me in all of the things that will benefit me when I don't even know to ask for them. I want to glorify God with my life and bring other people good, so I pray You will help me do this.

58

The Filling Spirit

Do not get drunk with wine,
for that is dissipation, but be filled with the Spirit.
EPHESIANS 5:18

ADORATION

Father, Your glory is my goal. Your praise is what I pursue. I want my life to serve as a testimony for how great You are. You've given me so many wonderful blessings, and one of them is the presence of the Holy Spirit in me.

The Holy Spirit enables me to do more than I ever could on my own. The Holy Spirit guides me on the path that will bring about good and peace and purpose. The Holy Spirit keeps me company when I feel alone and gives me wisdom on how to live with the right perspective. I praise You for the gift of the Holy Spirit and the opportunity to be filled by Him.

CONFESSION

God, I confess that over the years I've chosen to fill myself with many things. Things like material items or pleasures. Things that fill my mind with thoughts contrary to Your Word, such as with what I've chosen to watch for entertainment. Yet You've offered me the pure and powerful Holy Spirit, who can fill me with Your love.

Forgive me for the times I've crowded out the Holy Spirit. Forgive me for failing to walk in the fullness of the filling of the Holy Spirit. Create in me a clean heart so that I may depend on the Holy Spirit for my filling each day.

THANKSGIVING

Father, thank You for the Holy Spirit, who fills me with Your presence. Thank You for the Holy Spirit, who guides me and guards me. I want to walk according to the filling of the Holy Spirit. When I do, I am directed by Him. I'm influenced by Him. I'm made new by Him. Thank You that Your patience and grace extend to me in so many ways, including this offer to fill me with Your presence through the filling of the Holy Spirit.

Jesus Christ's sacrifice has made the filling of the Holy Spirit available to me. Thank You, Jesus, for Your great sacrifice.

SUPPLICATION

Lord God, I ask that You fill me with the fullness of the Holy Spirit. Help me walk according to the Holy Spirit and not lean on my own ways and thoughts.

Holy Spirit, guide me, direct me, and show me how to live a life pleasing to the Lord. Fill me with Your love, grace, patience, and joy. I want to know what it means to walk according to the will of God. Fill me with wisdom and strength. Fill me with all I need to live as a kingdom disciple honoring God in every way. I invite You to fill me and to convict me of anything I need to remove from my thoughts or actions because it's displeasing to Him.

59

The Spirit Who Distributes Gifts

*One and the same Spirit works all these things,
distributing to each one individually just as He wills.*
1 CORINTHIANS 12:11

ADORATION

Father, Your wise plan has considered all things. You've created gifts of the Holy Spirit for each of us to have and carry out. In this way, we bless one another and build up the body of Christ.

I worship You for Your wisdom and knowledge and the way You've designed Your Spirit to grace us with gifts. The Spirit works all these things and distributes to each one spiritual gifts as He wills. The Holy Spirit is to be praised for His will and the carrying out of the distribution of gifts in the body of Christ.

CONFESSION

God, I confess that I may not know all the spiritual gifts You've given me. And those I do know, I may not have fully realized or actualized in my life.

Forgive me for neglecting the nurturing of the spiritual gifts You've given me. I want to live my highest purpose and fulfill the destiny You've designed me to carry out. Help me to not neglect my gifts any longer. Rather, through Your great forgiveness, help me understand what a gift I've been given not only in the presence of the Holy Spirit but also in His distribution of spiritual gifts to me. Let Your love cleanse me and make my heart pure as snow.

THANKSGIVING

Father, thank You for the many spiritual gifts You've created for the Holy Spirit to distribute to the body of Christ. I know I'm blessed by these gifts and benefit from them, as do others. Each gift has been given in order to provide a certain amount of good and productivity to the community.

Thank You for the spiritual gifts You've given me so that I can be of service not only to You but also to others. I want to use my spiritual gifts in a way that honors You, Lord, and that demonstrates my heart of gratitude for all You've done and are doing for me. I bless Your name and thank You for the gift of the Holy Spirit.

SUPPLICATION

Lord God, I ask for greater insight into what my spiritual gifts are. Show me how I can better use them to be a blessing to others. I want to understand how I am to use my gifts in a more productive way. I want to know what Your plan is for my life and how my gifts interlace with this plan.

Holy Spirit, the gifts You've distributed to me are for good. Guide me on how to use them. Show me how best to make the most of them. Instruct me on my role in the overarching plan of God made manifest in the body of Jesus Christ, His church.

60

The Spirit Who Walks with You

Walk by the Spirit, and you will not carry out the desire of the flesh.

GALATIANS 5:16

ADORATION

Father, Your will has been made known to me through the presence of the Holy Spirit. Through these many prayers related to the names of the Holy Spirit, I've come to know You and see Your heart of love more clearly. You are a caring Father who's given me all I need to carry out Your will. I look to You to guide me with the Holy Spirit, who walks with me along the way. When I walk by the Spirit, I don't carry out the desire of my flesh. When I look to the Spirit to lead me, my flesh no longer controls me.

I honor You with my life, and I want to serve You in all I do. Make me a kingdom follower who pleases You in all things so that I can feel Your pleasure as I live my purpose and bring You glory.

CONFESSION

God, I confess that my flesh has guided me and directed me more than I should have ever allowed. I confess that I've leaned on my flesh as my guide instead of looking to the Spirit, who's been given to me to walk with me.

Forgive me for my thoughts that raise up contrary to Your revealed Word and truth. Forgive me for the pride in my heart that encourages me to walk according to my own path and to seek my own gain. Have mercy on me so that I can follow You freely, according to that which will bring about my greatest good and advance Your glory among those who follow You and throughout the entire world.

THANKSGIVING

Father, thank You for Your loving care. Thank You for teaching me about the Holy Spirit through this book of prayers based on His names and attributes. Thank You for encouraging me toward greater spiritual growth. Your blessings in my life are manifold, and I should never fail to thank You for each one.

You have been so kind to me, revealing the greater gifts and guidance of the Holy Spirit. The Holy Spirit walks with me, and I walk with Him. Where He goes, I should follow, as He knows Your mind and heart, Lord. He can lead me along the greatest path for Your glory and the expansion of Your kingdom agenda on earth.

SUPPLICATION

Lord God, I ask for the Spirit to nudge me when I've forgotten He's near so that I can remember to walk with Him and not go my own way. My own way only leads to destruction. My own thoughts and will only lead to consequences of no end. Apart from Your mercy and guidance, I don't know the right way to go. Show me what the right steps are so that I can walk in them.

Holy Spirit, guide me and take my hand as we walk together. Pull me close to You so that I won't stray. As I stay near to You, I am guided and directed toward goodness and God. Make me an instrument of Your glory and purpose so that others may come to know You and honor You as You deserve. Holy Spirit, glorify the Father through Your work in me.

A Look at the Fruit of the Spirit

Have you ever wondered why Christians still struggle with sin? Maybe you thought walking with Christ meant you would no longer be tempted by the desires of your flesh. I'm sorry to say this, but unfortunately, this is simply not true. As humans, our flesh will always have a desire to sin. But don't feel defeated! There's good news. Our heavenly Father has sent us the help we need to beat the temptations of our earthly, fleshly desires—the Holy Spirit.

Galatians 5:16 (NIV)—*"Walk by the Spirit, and you will not gratify the desires of the flesh."*

Having a complete understanding of this concept of "walking by the Spirit" will change your life. So let's take a closer look at what it means and how we can apply it to our lives.

If you've come to relationship with Christ, something magnificent has occurred. That is, the Spirit of God has taken up residence in your life, given you a new nature, and placed the new nature in your old, fleshly body. That means there's a war going on between the two—your flesh and your new, Christ-given nature.

But you have the ability to walk in the Spirit when you allow the Holy Spirit to lead the way. When the Spirit takes over, you function by relationship. You can't win the war between your new nature and your flesh by following a list of dos and don'ts. Instead, as you grow in true relationship with the Spirit, your desire to follow Christ will outweigh your flesh's desire for sin.

Now here's the key: God doesn't expect you to win this fight alone. He's given His Holy Spirit to help.

It's like in a football game: Another team is opposing you, and you have to face their opposition. As you're trying to go forward in your Christian life, this other team (the flesh) is ready to tackle you in the backfield. In football, there's a pulling guard. When the halfback receives the ball and it's going to swoop right, instead of blocking the man in front of him, that guard will pull in front of the halfback. We call this running interference. So when the opposing team seeks to tackle the halfback, he has somebody in front of him to resist their attempts.

Friends, God has given you a pulling guard—the Holy Spirit! The Spirit of God is designed to run interference so that even though the temptations of sin want to tackle you, they can't, because you're being led and protected by the Spirit.

So, yes, while it's true that you and I are engaged in a conflict between our flesh and our spirit, I want you to remember that there is victory. When we submit our desires to the will of Christ, we're no longer obligated to fulfill the desires of our flesh. This doesn't cancel the desires, but the Holy Spirit gives us the power to overcome them, to overcome our sinful nature.

How do you know if you're walking in the Spirit? You don't have to wonder whether your actions are spiritual or fleshly. Scripture says if they're fleshly, you'll know it. It's evident. The Christian life does not require guesswork.

Galatians 5:19-21 (NIV)— *"The acts of the flesh are obvious: sexual immorality, impurity and debauchery; idolatry and witchcraft; hatred, discord,* *jealousy, fits of rage, selfish ambition, dissensions, factions and envy; drunkenness, orgies, and the like. I warn you, as I did before, that those who live like this will not inherit the kingdom of God."*

Now, just as the flesh is evident, so is the Spirit. God says that the Spirit gives fruit.

Galatians 5:22-23 (NIV)—*"The fruit of the Spirit is love, joy, peace, forbearance, kindness, goodness, faithfulness, gentleness and self-control."*

Let me tell you three things you need to know about fruit:

1. *Fruit is always visible.* Watch out for any tree in your backyard that gives you invisible fruit. In fact, the bigger the fruit you see is, the riper and more luxurious it appears.

2. *Fruit always reflects the character of the tree.* If it's an apple tree, it will produce apples. If it's an orange grove, it will produce oranges. If it's a pear tree, it will produce pears. If it's a vineyard, it will produce grapes. So you won't get oranges growing on apple trees or pears growing on orange trees. The fruit that comes out of a life controlled by the Spirit will reflect the character of Jesus Christ. Christlikeness will eventuate from your life.

3. *Fruit is always borne for the benefit of someone else.* Fruit that exists only for itself grows rotten. You never see fruit chewing on itself. The fruit of the Spirit is always God-centered. It's always God-oriented. Whereas the flesh is always self-centered, the fruit of the Spirit is focused on others.

What Are the Fruit of the Spirit Like?

Love. Love is the ability to seek the glory of God in the life of somebody else. When we say, "You're not loving me," that's the flesh. But when we say, "Even if you aren't loving me, let me show you what real love looks like," that's the Spirit.

Joy. Happiness is circumstantially driven. In other words, if you give me good times, I'll be happy. But joy has nothing to do with happiness. Joy has to do with the well on the inside, not the circumstances on the outside. It's the overflow of the life of God within.

Peace. God says the Spirit can bring harmony where there's conflict. He can give two very different personalities the ability to live together in peace. He can bring groups at war together in harmony.

Patience (or forbearance). The Spirit gives you the ability to view circumstances and challenges through the lens of God's sovereignty, helping you wait on His perfect timing and way.

Kindness. The Spirit causes you to think of how you can be of help to those around you.

Goodness. This goodness comprises deeds that benefit, not deeds that destroy.

Faithfulness. You are faithful when the Spirit allows you to be constant and consistent in your Christian walk.

Gentleness (or meekness). This means the Spirit gives you a willingness to submit to the will of God even if it's not your preference.

Self-control. Self-control is the ability to say no to wrong no matter how nice it seems and yes to right.

Galatians 5:23 (NIV)—*"Against such things there is no law."*

The beauty of walking in the Spirit is that we don't need a law to allow us to do it. We need the Holy Spirit. So if we're going to live this Christian life, it seems to me that we would want to get all of the Holy

Spirit we can get! Better yet, let the Holy Spirit have all of us that He can get. Right?

When I was growing up in Baltimore, I played in front of the neighborhood's open fire hydrant and found it fascinating that it never ran out of water. I had no idea how that little three-foot fire hydrant could hold all that. That is, until my father explained that underneath the ground was a hookup to a reservoir, and the reservoir had more water than I could ever use. So as long as there was this invisible hookup, there would always be an outflow from the hydrant.

You and I are hydrants. The Holy Spirit is the dam. As long as we stay hooked up, the water will continue to flow.

Galatians 5:25—*"If we live by the Spirit, let us also walk by the Spirit."*

Here are three things you need to know about what it means to walk by the Spirit:

1. *Walking always assumes you're going somewhere.* If you're going to walk by the Spirit, you must commit yourself to the will of God. Commit yourself to the direction God wants you to go in your life.

2. *Walking assumes continuous movement.* Have you ever seen a baby learning to walk? They're unstable and fall down. But we don't condemn them for falling down, because they get up and try again. Something is wrong if they don't. So if you blow it, don't stay there. Get up and keep going.

3. *Walking means dependence.* When you walk, you place your weight on your legs one at a time. It means you're resting on something (or someone) to hold you up. So, friends, every time your flesh wants to do what's selfish and ungodly, call on the Spirit of God to help you at that moment. Don't depend

on what you prayed when you started your day. Call on Him for His power to give you victory right then and there. Remember, "Greater is He who is in you than he who is in the world" (1 John 4:4).

APPENDIX B:

The Urban Alternative

The Urban Alternative (TUA) equips, empowers, and unites Christians to impact individuals, families, churches, and communities through a thoroughly kingdom-agenda worldview. In teaching truth, we seek to transform lives.

The core cause of the problems we face in our personal lives, homes, churches, and societies is a spiritual one. Therefore, the only way to address that core cause is spiritually. We've tried a political, social, economic, and even a religious agenda, and now it's time for a kingdom agenda.

The kingdom agenda can be defined as the visible manifestation of the comprehensive rule of God over every area of life.

The unifying central theme throughout the Bible is the glory of God and the advancement of His kingdom. The conjoining thread from Genesis to Revelation—from beginning to end—is focused on one thing: God's glory through advancing God's kingdom.

When we do not recognize that theme, the Bible becomes for us a series of disconnected stories that are great for inspiration but seem to be unrelated in purpose and direction. Understanding the role of the kingdom in Scripture increases our understanding of the relevancy of this several-thousand-year-old text to our day-to-day living. That's because God's kingdom was not only then; it is now.

The absence of the kingdom's influence in our personal lives, family lives, churches, and communities has led to a deterioration in our world of immense proportions:

- People live segmented, compartmentalized lives because they lack God's kingdom worldview.

- Families disintegrate because they exist for their own satisfaction rather than for the kingdom.

- Churches are limited in the scope of their impact because they fail to comprehend that the goal of the church is not the church itself but the kingdom.

- Communities have nowhere to turn to find real solutions for real people who have real problems because the church has become divided, in-grown, and unable to transform the cultural and political landscape in any relevant way.

By optimizing the solutions of heaven, the kingdom agenda offers us a way to see and live life with a solid hope. When God is no longer the final and authoritative standard under which all else falls, order and hope have left with Him. But the reverse of that is true as well: as long as we have God, we have hope. If God is still in the picture, and as long as His agenda is still on the table, it's not over.

Even if relationships collapse, God will sustain us. Even if finances dwindle, God will keep us. Even if dreams die, God will revive us. As long as God and His rule are still the overarching standard in our lives, families, churches, and communities, there is always hope.

Our world needs the King's agenda. Our churches need the King's agenda. Our families need the King's agenda.

We've put together a three-part plan to direct us to heal the divisions and strive for unity as we move toward the goal of truly being one nation under God. This three-part plan calls us to assemble with others in unity, to address the issues that divide us, and to act together for social impact. Following this plan, we will see individuals, families, churches, and communities transformed as we follow God's kingdom agenda in every area of our lives. You can request this plan by texting the keyword "strategy" to 55659 or visiting TonyEvans.org/strategy.

In many major cities, drivers can take a loop to the other side of the city when they don't want to head straight through downtown. This loop takes them close enough to the city center so they can see its towering buildings and skyline but not close enough to actually experience it.

This is precisely what we, as a culture, have done with God. We have put Him on the "loop" of our personal, family, church, and community lives. He's close enough to be at hand should we need Him in an emergency but far enough away that He can't be the center of who we are. We want God on the "loop," not the King of the Bible who comes downtown into the very heart of our ways. And as we have seen in our own lives and in the lives of others, leaving God on the "loop" brings about dire consequences.

But when we make God, and His rule, the centerpiece of all we think, do, or say, we experience Him in the way He longs for us to experience Him. He wants us to be kingdom people with kingdom minds set on fulfilling His kingdom's purposes. He wants us to pray, as Jesus did, "Not My will, but Thy will be done" because His is the kingdom, the power, and the glory.

There is only one God, and we are not Him. As King and Creator, God calls the shots. Only when we align ourselves under His comprehensive hand will we access His full power and authority in all spheres of life: personal, familial, ecclesiastical, and governmental.

As we learn how to govern ourselves under God, we then transform the institutions of family, church, and society using a biblically based kingdom worldview.

Under Him, we touch heaven and change earth.

To achieve our goal, we use a variety of strategies, approaches, and resources for reaching and equipping as many people as possible.

BROADCAST MEDIA

Millions of individuals experience *The Alternative with Dr. Tony Evans*, a daily broadcast on nearly 2,000 radio outlets and in more than 130 countries. The broadcast can also be seen on several television networks including TBN and Fox Business and is available online at TonyEvans. org. You can also listen to or view the daily broadcast by downloading the Tony Evans app for free in the App Store. More than 60,000,000 message downloads/streams occur each year.

LEADERSHIP TRAINING

The *Tony Evans Training Center* (TETC) facilitates a comprehensive discipleship platform, which provides an educational program that embodies the ministry philosophy of Dr. Tony Evans as expressed through the kingdom agenda. The training courses focus on leadership development and discipleship in the following five tracks:

1. Bible and Theology

2. Individual Spiritual Growth

3. Family and Relationship

4. Church Health and Leadership Development

5. Society and Community Impact Strategies

The TETC program includes courses for both local and online students. Furthermore, TETC programming includes course work for nonstudent attendees. Pastors, Christian leaders, and Christian laity—both local and at a distance—can seek out the Kingdom Agenda Certificate for personal, spiritual, and professional development. For more information, visit TonyEvansTraining.org.

Kingdom Agenda Pastors (KAP) provides a viable network for likeminded pastors who embrace the kingdom agenda philosophy. Pastors have the opportunity to go deeper with Dr. Tony Evans as they are given greater biblical knowledge, practical applications, and resources to impact individuals, families, churches, and communities. KAP welcomes senior and associate pastors of all churches. KAP also offers an annual Summit held each year in Dallas with intensive seminars, workshops, and resources. For more information, visit KAFellowship.org.

Pastors' Wives Ministry, founded by the late Dr. Lois Evans, provides counsel, encouragement, and spiritual resources for pastors' wives as they serve with their husbands in the ministry. A primary focus of the ministry is the KAP Summit, where senior pastors' wives have a safe place to reflect, renew, and relax along with receiving training in personal development, spiritual growth, and care for their emotional and physical wellbeing. For more information, visit LoisEvans.org.

KINGDOM COMMUNITY IMPACT

The outreach programs of The Urban Alternative seek to provide positive impact on individuals, churches, families, and communities through a variety of ministries. We see these efforts as necessary to our calling as a ministry and essential to the communities we serve. With training on how to initiate and maintain programs to adopt schools, provide homeless services, and partner toward unity and justice with the local police precincts, which creates a connection between the police and our community, we, as a ministry, live out God's kingdom agenda according to our *Kingdom Strategy for Community Transformation*.

The *Kingdom Strategy for Community Transformation* is a three-part plan that equips churches to have a positive impact on their communities for the kingdom of God. It also provides numerous practical suggestions for how this three-part plan can be implemented in your community, and it serves as a blueprint for unifying churches around the common goal of creating a better world for all of us. For more information, visit TonyEvans.org, then click on the link to access the 3-Point Plan. A course for this strategy is also offered online through the Tony Evans Training Center.

Tony Evans Films ushers in positive life change through compelling video-shorts, animation, and feature-length films. We seek to build kingdom disciples through the power of story. We use a variety of platforms for viewer consumption and have 220,000,000+ digital views. We also merge video-shorts and film with relevant Bible study materials to bring people to the saving knowledge of Jesus Christ and to strengthen the body of Christ worldwide. Tony Evans Films released its first feature-length film, *Kingdom Men Rising*, in April 2019 in more than 800 theaters nationwide in partnership with Lifeway Films. The second release, *Journey with Jesus*, is in partnership with RightNow Media and was released for three nights of nearly 1,000 sold-out theaters in November 2021. The third release is *Unbound: The Bible's Journey Through History*, a documentary focusing on the transmission of the Bible from the third through the sixteenth centuries.

RESOURCE DEVELOPMENT

By providing a variety of published materials, we are fostering lifelong learning partnerships with the people we serve. Dr. Evans has published more than 125 unique titles based on more than 50 years of preaching—in booklet, book, or Bible study format. He also holds the honor of writing and publishing the first full-Bible commentary and study Bible by an African American, released in 2019. This Bible sits in permanent display as a historic release in the Museum of the Bible in Washington, DC.

For more information, and to opt-in to Dr. Evans' devotional email, text the word "DEVO" to 55659, call (800) 800-3222, or visit us online at:

WWW.TONYEVANS.ORG/DEVO

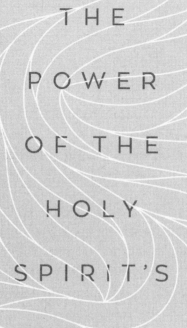

THE
POWER
OF THE
HOLY
SPIRIT'S
NAMES

TONY EVANS

KNOW THE SPIRIT THROUGH HIS NAMES

Living Water. Helper. Lord. Many believers long for a clearer understanding of the Holy Spirit and the role He plays in our relationship with God. The good news is, when we study the Bible, the Spirit's specific identity and work as a member of the Trinity is made clear.

In *The Power of The Holy Spirit's Names*, bestselling author and pastor Dr. Tony Evans examines 12 of the Spirit's most significant titles and what they reveal about this powerful, present, and personal expression of the triune God. As you read, you'll gain eye-opening insights into how the Spirit moves within the hearts of believers while learning how His indwelling of you shapes your unique faith.

As we grow in our ability to love, revere, and relate to the person of the Holy Spirit, we also grow in our capacity to experience God. This book will help you internalize profound truths about the Holy Spirit's character and transform how you understand the Trinity.

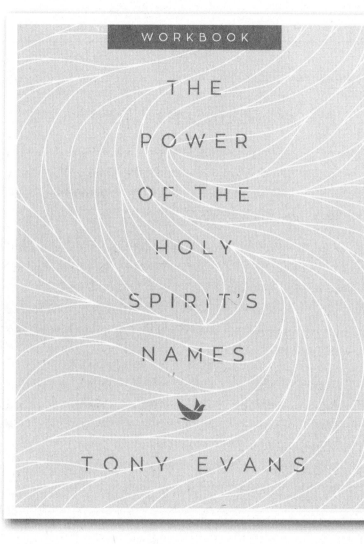

THE POWER OF THE HOLY SPIRIT'S NAMES

TONY EVANS

WHO IS THE HOLY SPIRIT?

The Holy Spirit plays the incredible role of both empowering the individual believer and the church—and as you study this awe-inspiring identity of the Trinity's third member, you gain a clearer understanding of our omnipotent triune God.

With *The Power of the Holy Spirit's Names Workbook*, Dr. Tony Evans leads you on an in-depth exploration of the Spirit's characteristics, duties, and mission among mankind. You'll take a closer look at some of the titles of the Spirit examined in *The Power of the Holy Spirit's Names* and appreciate how He influences and inspires your faith in Christ.

Written to be used in tandem with *The Power of the Holy Spirit's Names DVD*, this guide provides a dynamic growth experience for individuals and small groups alike. Let this workbook help you discover profound and uplifting truths about the One described in Scripture as *Wind and Fire*, *Intercessor*, and *Power*.

THE

POWER

OF THE

HOLY

SPIRIT'S

NAMES

TONY EVANS

ANSWERS TO YOUR QUESTIONS
ABOUT THE HOLY SPIRIT

With this DVD companion to *The Power of the Holy Spirit's Names Workbook*, you'll dive deeper into the incredible revelations the Bible makes about the Holy Spirit's unique role, identity, and work. As you watch this fascinating sermon series from bestselling author and pastor Dr. Tony Evans, you'll continue your journey of drawing nearer to each member of the Trinity.

Perfect for group or individual study, *The Power of the Holy Spirit's Names DVD* illuminates one of the most central yet under-discussed parts of the Christian faith. You'll grow in understanding, reverence, and love for the complete Trinity as you examine the essential and personal role the Holy Spirit plays in your relationship with God.

To learn more about Harvest House books and
to read sample chapters, visit our website:

www.HarvestHousePublishers.com

HARVEST HOUSE PUBLISHERS
EUGENE, OREGON